Messiah
in America
Moyshe Nadir

2018 Farlag Press

Farlag is a registered non-profit based in France / Association loi 1901.

ISBN 9791096677047

Achevé d'imprimer par Lightning Source à Milton Keynes (Royaume-uni)

Dépot légal : Août 2018

Association Farlag :

17 Cours. J. F. Kennedy — Rennes 35000

www.farlag.com

Messiah
in America

Moyshe Nadir

A Drama in Five Acts

Translated by
Michael Shapiro

CONTENTS

Introduction   8

Translator's note   14

Messiah in America   18

Notes   124

THE MESSIAH ARRIVES:
AN INTRODUCTION TO NADIR'S SATIRIC THEATRE

Joel Schechter

Where I come from, in the world of theatre, you often hear references to playwriting that is "Shakespearean" in its poetic language and breadth, or "Brechtian" in its political engagement, or "Beckettian" in its grim, existential humour. I would like to recommend another adjective to the world of literature, this one coined in April, 1926, by *Frayhayt* drama critic Robert Yukelson. He found a Yiddish play to be "Moyshenadirish," which is not surprising, considering that Moyshe Nadir wrote the play under discussion. The term connotes a playful, Puckish attitude toward the world; but that playfulness cannot be separated from Nadir's anti-religious and anti-capitalistic satires, some of which deserve to be celebrated today along with their author's name.

Moyshe Nadir was a pseudonym chosen by the American Yiddish writer Isaac Reiss, originally born in Galicia in 1885. He arrived in America at the age of thirteen, and within a few years was writing poems, drama reviews, and satires for leading Yiddish journals. The pseudonym Nadir, or "*Na dir*," as in "take this," or "take this and choke on it," embodies some of the daring and acid humour his work repeatedly offered readers in leftist Yiddish publications—the *Frayhayt, Hamer* and *Signal*—during the 1920s and 30s.

Even before Yukelson called his work "Moyshenadirish" in 1926, the satirist was quite well known in Yiddish literary circles. But at that time he had not yet written some of his best plays and poems. In the Thirties, Nadir's satire had much in common with the work of a few other gifted New York Yiddish artists—puppeteers Yosl Cutler and Zuni Maud, visual artist Bill Gropper, the Federal Theatre Project's Yiddish vaudeville troupe, and Artef (Arbeter Teater Farband, or Worker's Theatrical Alliance) director Benno Schneider, all of whom became his collaborators.

When he called a play "Moyshenadirish," Yukelson was reviewing Maud and Cutler's Modicut puppet theatre premiere of *The Other World*. The staging of a script by Nadir featured a golden-bearded divinity lording it over the archangel Gabriel and other inhabitants of the next world. Which is not to say Nadir believed in the next world; his portrait of that realm in the puppet play suggests there is no more justice, charity or compassion in the Other World than on earth. The Lord demands praise from his subjects, and a parody of Jewish prayers surfaces in a litany offered to the Other World's ruler, who displays high self-esteem, to put it mildly, in this anti-religious satire.

GOD'S VOICE: Hey, Gabriel.
GABRIEL *(trembling with fear):* His voice! *(Subservient.)* What do you need, God?
GOD: Who's great?
GABRIEL: You.
GOD: Who's mighty?
GABRIEL: You.
GOD: Who's eternal?

GABRIEL: You.

GOD: How do you know?

GABRIEL: You told me so yourself.

GOD: That's correct.

GABRIEL: All day long. All day long. He bores us with these stupid questions. And we have to answer. What can you do? He's in charge. Ech. God help me if I can get out of here. *(Off.)*

Translation: Michael Shapiro

I once heard the late Yiddish writer and editor Itche Goldberg, who knew Nadir personally, quote these lines as a sample of Nadir's comic sensibility. Goldberg knew the lines by heart, and smiled as he recited them. The puppet play rightly struck Robert Yukelson as "Moyshenadirish," meaning (in my reading of his Yiddish), playful or pranksterish to the highest degree. You might even say its iconoclastic humour reaches to the heavens.

Today Nadir's plays, Yiddish *feuilletons*, and his epic poetry remain largely out of print, and untranslated in English. That is one reason to celebrate the arrival of his Messiah in Michael Shapiro's new translation. (Earlier excerpts from the play appeared in translations by Nahma Sandrow and Harvey Fink, who also deserve recognition for their attention to Nadir's comedy and excerpts of the current translation appeared in *Pakn Treger*.) The prankster whom Yukelson praised deserves to be known beyond the world of Yiddish and Jewish studies. He was a satirist in the tradition of Aristophanes, Ben Jonson, and S.J. Perelman; but unlike those other wits, Nadir satirised modern capitalism and traditional messianism in some of his exemplary

works. In a book (*Messiahs of 1933*) I have written at greater length about his masterful play, *Messiah in America*,
and *Rivington Street*, his epic and politically-charged poem
about New York's Lower East Side. Now that the Messiah
play can easily be accessed in its new English translation, I
am hopeful that more will be written about it, and perhaps
it will even be staged again, and taught in dramatic literature courses. It first appeared on stage in 1933, directed
by Benno Schneider for the Artef Studio in New York. Nadir's friend Yosl Cutler designed the sets. The limited-run
presentation appeared at selected tour sites, such as the
East New York Worker's Club, at 608 Cleveland Street, on
May 27th; aside from press advertisements for the work,
few other notices discussed the work, which received far
less attention than Artef's larger and famous productions
(such as *200,000*, based on the writing of Sholem Aleichem).
The Yiddish text was printed by Freiheit Publishing in a
1932 collection of Nadir's plays. It has been staged again
in recent years, both in English and in Yiddish. *Meshiekh
in Amerike* was performed in May 2012 by the New Yiddish Rep at the Hebrew Actors' Union building, 31 East 7th
Street, NYC. It was directed by Moshe Yassur and adapted
by Shane Baker.

Regrettably, this satire and others by Nadir remain timely
decades after he wrote them. American troubles with
immigration, income inequality, racial and religious dis-
crimination continue, in old, new and sometimes violent
forms. (Nadir himself portrays some disturbing racist be-
havior in one Messiah scene; the cruelty shown should not
be mistaken for an endorsement of it.) His remarkable comedy about false messiahs hired by theatre producers also
mocks the excesses of monopoly capital, religious fervour,

celebrity worship, and sports extravaganzas all in one play, quite a feat. While Nadir's theatre producers in the play sell tickets to those who would see the Messiah on stage, or in a boxing ring, today Americans audiences would not have to leave their homes to see the latest miracle worker (i.e. —political candidate, athlete, evangelical, salesman); they can watch on a cablecast or an iPhone, with commercials (more sales pitches) included.

It could be argued that in our time we have more false messiahs and more celebrity worship of questionable kinds than existed in Nadir's day. The current President of the United States—Donald Trump—was called a false messiah in a November 2016 article in the Yiddish *Forverts* A producer of Nadir's play might want to revise the text slightly, adjust its references to the enormities now visible in American politics and media spectacle. But the playwright's original dramatic structure, his plot and characters remain wildly "Moyshenadirish," which is to say his humour contains within it a welcome, playful secular wariness of blind faith and self-serving excesses.

The excesses of misguided faith within the play had an unfortunate counterpart in Nadir's own admitted "worship" of Soviet leaders for several decades, a more or less blind faith he renounced in writing around the time of the Hitler-Stalin pact. His pro-Communist leanings cost him friends and followers over the years; but his political consciousness of a world in which breadlines, unemployment, plutocratic wealth and profitable war preparations co-existed led Nadir to write some of his most resourceful and appealing satiric creations. The world which he saw troubled by economic disaster, injustice, prejudice and false messiahs in modern dress, is still too much with us for Moyshe Nadir's satiric writing and activism to be forgotten. Until another, better Messiah arrives, we ought to welcome this one's comic return.

Joel Schechter is Professor of Theatre Arts at San Francisco State University. A version of this introduction appeared in his book Radical Yiddish, *published by Jewish Currents.*

Translator's Note

I first became aware of *Messiah in America* through the work of Joel Schechter. Learning about this play and about the Modicut Theater convinced me that I needed to get serious about learning Yiddish. Work like this was too good, too hilarious to pass up. And there was another connection. I grew up in Woodside, Queens, a neighborhood with a sprinkling of Communists and ex-Communists carefully hiding their past. With McCarthy breathing down their necks, who could blame them? And so, growing up, I heard little about the radical Yiddish Lower East Side my parents had left behind. Learning about these plays, almost certainly attended by my parents in their former lives, felt like getting the stories your parents wouldn't tell you. In fact, it *was* getting the stories your parents wouldn't tell you.

When they left behind the radical Yiddish Lower East Side, they not only left behind a culture and context that had sustained them, they left behind the language as well. And so, we need translations. Translating this play has been a joy and a labour of love. As a translator, I felt my remit was to give you, the reader, what Moyshe Nadir gave me. For the most part, I felt able to stay close to both the literal meaning and the spirit of the text. I have tried to produce something as sarcastic, as incisive, as outrageous and as fun as the original, whether read from the page or read from the stage. But we can't have the same experience as Moyshe Nadir's audience. His audience had a frame of reference halfway between the old country and the new, mixing a radical modernist viewpoint with a traditional religious background. This play is steeped in its time. I hope the endnotes will bring more of this to hand for modern readers.

Moyshe Nadir's audience also saw this play against the backdrop of the economic and political crises of the day, including the rise of fascism in Europe and the fear fascism could come to America through the likes of Huey Long and Father Coughlin. Sadly, we once again share this fear. The current moment looks darker than any other in my life, a life that has included the rise of McCarthy and the assassinations of Malcolm X, King and two Kennedys. At the time of *Messiah,* McCarthy was still far in the future. He used to be in our past, but is once more front and center with Roy Cohn's protegé occupying the White House. The reader will sadly find much in this play that is evergreen. Mr. Zipkin, aka Scoundrel Johnnie, aka "Zip", a sideshow operator and all-around swindler says, "[T]he dimes become dollars, and the dollars become hundreds, and the hundreds become millions. And if you've got a million, you're alright. And with a couple of million, I, 'Zip', can be President of America, President of the richest republic in the world." Wilfred Owen tells us, "All a poet can do today is warn." Moyshe Nadir warned. The rest is up to us.

Many people helped make this book possible. I wish to thank Mary Kerins for her support and encouragement. Mary and Daniel Shapiro both helped to underwrite this effort. Thanks go to Jean Oggins who first pointed me to the work of Joel Schechter, to Ellie Kellman and her students who welcomed me into their midst, to Alex Green, formerly of Back Pages Books, who helped me to keep focus, and to Daniel Wuenschel who is ever a good spirit for a creative project. Sholem Beinfeld's depth of knowledge of the language and the era proved indispensable. Thanks also go to Jacob Rabinowitz, friend of many years and wizard of many languages.

A NOTE ON TRANSLITERATION: The great Yiddish teacher, Pesach Fishman used to say, with some irritation, "Don't ask me what's the right way to spell a Yiddish word in English. It's not in English." But of course some Yiddish words become English while others are just visiting. To a large extent I have tried to follow YIVO transliteration, but set it aside according to personal taste. A prime example is the character who is here spelled Menachem-Joseph. YIVO spelling would have him as Menakhem-Yosef, better phonetically, but a bit uncomfortable to my English-speaking eye. So I beg you to pronounce it correctly while allowing me to spell it incorrectly.

CHARACTERS

MENACHEM-JOSEF
JACKIE BLUFFER
JIM, a photographer (later, "The Bearded Lady")
FLOSSIE, a typist
GREY, BLACK, YELLOW, reporters[1]
HUNCHBACK
REB SIMCHA, Messiah for men
DR. KESTLEBERG, new Messiah for women
SCOUNDREL JOHNNIE, MR. ZIPKIN (later, "ZIP")
CHARLIE (later "THE BARKER")

SETTING

We see the office of MENACHEM-JOSEF, *a* luftmentsh, *a real Menachem-Mendel,[2] dealing with theatre generally and an assortment of artsy trinkets and religious gew-gaws. The same* MENACHEM-JOSEF *stands ready to deal in kosher pork or* treyf[3] *mezuzahs if there's a dollar in it. The main thing: "It should make a racket."*

Doors right and left lead to side offices. The desk is littered with books, newspapers, clippings. On the walls, portraits of all sorts of celebrities, from Jack Dempsey to Dr. Chaim Weizmann, Morris Schwartz and Mendel Beiliss.[4] Two phones on the desk, one small, light-coloured: a love phone; the other, large, black, ominous: it means business. A table with a typewriter. A closet with alphabetised shelves. Smoky, dingy, with a small window that looks out God knows where.

Translator's Note: much of the original dialogue is in English, which I have rendered *in slant*. While the characters speak Yiddish as a native language, they speak English with an accent. We are then in the slightly paradoxical situation where the characters should speak what was in Yiddish as unaccented English and what was in English with a slight Yiddish accent.

Prologue

Pulcinella-Mask declaims loudly in front of the curtain in an assortment of Yiddish styles.

Good evening friends, good evening! Let there be no doubt,
I'll show you what theatre's about!
The land of the savvy, the Kingdom of Gold
In cheeriest colours, its story unfolds.
In the land of the dollar, Messiah's the goods,
Like herring, or oil or mushrooms from the woods.
Therefore, good friends, be ready to hear
The nice little feast we've prepared for your ears.
With fat, salt and cinnamon we've cooked a nice stew
To cram down the throats of treyf Bolsheviks like you!

(In an elevated, distinguished voice:)

I am the Prologue, polished and fine.
I'll be here with you just a little more time.
Then I disappear and others come next
Because too much appetizer would just make you retch.
And so, to your health, for again, there's no doubt
I'll show you what theatre's about!

(Tragic)

And why wear a mask? It's your face you should wear,

A mask hides what it can, a face hides what's there.
Life and theatre, who knows what they are?
Just a bit, I the Prologue, can tell you for sure—
No ship is ever as tall as its mast,
And what don't start good won't be good to the last.
So sit yourself comfy, to watch and to hear
As the gates of America open: The time's drawing near.
The Goddess of the Dollar lifts high her hand
And watches offshore, o'er the great Golden Land.

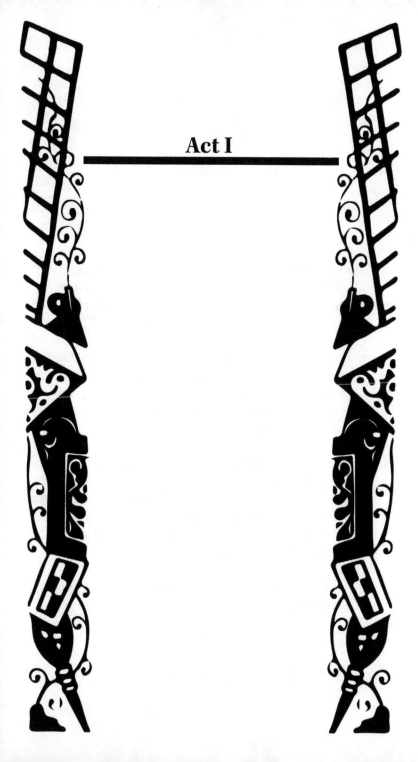

Act I

Act I

The curtain goes up. MENACHEM-JOSEF *sits at the table with his secretary* JACKIE BLUFFER, *a healthy, loud-mouthed boy with more balls than brains. Wears large, black-framed glasses.*

MENACHEM-JOSEF *(Has a large handsome graying head, a sick, restless, feverish, energetic face. He spits continuously as if he had something stuck to his lip):* It's gotta be new! It should make a racket! We haven't done anything new in a long time.

JACKIE: I had new business cards printed up for you, Mr. Menachem-Josef. You're really gonna like them. Here. *(Holds up a calling card.)* It's got a motto: *(reads from the card)* Menachem-Josef, Theatrical Producer, Number 32 Broadway, New York. *(To* MENACHEM-JOSEF*)* That's nothing. Read the motto.

BOTH *(Almost a duet):* "You can curse my mother, just remember my name."

JACKIE: So, do you like it?

MENACHEM-JOSEF: It's good. It's good. Bravo! *(Slaps Jack-*

ie on the back.) The main thing, y'unerstan me, it's gotta make a racket. It's gotta go beyond. You get it? You think I need the money? I don't have enough money? *(Sad.)* I have so little money. If that Scoundrel Johnnie has eighty-five thousand dollars, I've gotta have at least ninety thousand. Just to spite him, y'unerstan?

JACKIE: Of course I understand. My brains haven't shriveled. *(Flatteringly.)* Otherwise, how could I be your secretary? *(Kissing ass.)* A fellow needs his head screwed on to be your secretary.

MENACHEM-JOSEF: My wife always nags me. I work too much. I don't watch my health. What do you think? You don't think she's right, my wife? But it's not about living, it's about out-living the other guy. Y'unerstan? If Scoundrel Johnnie lives to be sixty, I've gotta live to sixty-one. And if he lives to 102, I've gotta live to 103. *(Remembers.)* Listen, what happened with that Swedish ballet, Jackie?

JACKIE: Nothing happened. They wanted too much money.

MENACHEM-JOSEF: There's no such thing as too much money in show business. The more money an artist gets, the greater he is. That's what the *(rolls his eyes)* discerning audience thinks. Ha ha! The great, aristocratic audience—They like to be swindled. Remember when I put on *The Golden Peacock*?[5] At first, nobody came. Remember, Jack? Tickets were cheap. And nobody came. And the musicians and the choir cost us a pile of money. So what did I do? I got rid of half the musicians, fired half the choir, doubled the price and they started coming.

(Differently.) The Swedish Ballet—how much did they want?

JACKIE: Thirty-two hundred a week and a guaranteed sixteen weeks.

MENACHEM-JOSEF: That's too much. Not worth it. Anyway, they're probably too good. American audiences won't like it. Whaddaya say? Maybe a woman that killed a few people? Or maybe a pretty girl who jumped from the twenty-first floor and didn't die.

JACKIE: There was a woman like that.

MENACHEM-JOSEF *(Perks up.):* What did she do?

JACKIE: She swallowed her own teeth. Three times already. The papers were full of it.

MENACHEM-JOSEF: Good. Bring her here. We'll put her name up in lights. Can she sing?

JACKIE: No.

MENACHEM-JOSEF: Can she dance?

JACKIE: No.

MENACHEM-JOSEF: Can she play an instrument?

JACKIE: Not that either.

MENACHEM-JOSEF: Can she walk a tightrope? Can she crochet a sock with her feet?

JACKIE: No.

MENACHEM-JOSEF: Is she pretty?

JACK: No. *(Unhappyily)* She can't do anything except swallow her teeth.

MENACHEM-JOSEF: In that case she'll be good for later in the season. Right now, early winter, we need something better. It's gotta grab 'em. It's gotta make a racket. Y'unerstan?

JACKIE *(Thinking):* I've got it!

MENACHEM-JOSEF: What?

JACKIE: A spitter!

MENACHEM-JOSEF: A spitter! What do you mean, a spitter?

JACKIE: It's something new. It's a guy who can spit further than anyone. His record is six metres.

MENACHEM-JOSEF: Six metres is no big deal. I think somebody's already spit further. He's been out-spit.

JACKIE *(Hurt):* What are you saying Mr. Menachem-Josef? Nobody's spit six metres. Except the Philadelphia Spitter. And that guy's dead.

MENACHEM-JOSEF *(Earnestly, philosophically):* That's how it is. The best in the land are all dying out. *(Pause.)* How much does he want?

JACKIE: The spitter? He charges 450 dollars a show. I think it's an honest living.

MENACHEM-JOSEF: If that's what he makes, that's what he earns, of course. There's no question. But for me, it's too much. I'm not in it for some cause here. It's not like I'm trying to bring the Messiah.

JACKIE *(Brought up sharp by the last word. Something's just occurred to him):* What did you say? Messiah? And why not bring the Messiah? If you can make a dollar, why not? How is the Messiah any worse than a Spitter?

MENACHEM-JOSEF: Is that just talk or do you mean business!

JACKIE: I mean business. *(Draws closer. Becomes fervent, eloquent.)* You see, it's like this: In America, we have a lot of Jews. In New York alone, we have God knows how many Jews. Am I right, or not?

MENACHEM-JOSEF: Right.

JACKIE: So. Good. Figure like this. Every Jew is waiting for the Messiah. And every Jew that's waiting for the Messiah can afford, let's say, a dollar seventy-five for a ticket.[6] Am I right, or not?

MENACHEM-JOSEF: Right!

JACKIE: Figure like this. Two thousand people a night at a dollar seventy five, we gross three thousand five hundred dollars a night. Am I right, or not?

MENACHEM-JOSEF: Right!

JACKIE: Figure like this: Seven shows a week, plus two matinees, Shabbos and Sunday, we have nine shows a week. At 3,500 dollars a show. That makes. . .

MENACHEM-JOSEF *(Cool and cautiously):* Wait. Let's shut the door. *(Does so, looking around to see if anyone's listening.)* All in all, I like it. Let's do it. But where are we going to get a Messiah?

JACKIE: Hang on. We'll get to that. Meanwhile, figure like this. *(Picks up a piece of paper. Computes, writes, erases, crumples up the used paper, throws it away.)* Besides the 3,500 dollars a show we can also have private redemptions, too. Every Jew who wants to be redeemed has to pay thirty-five dollars. Even better: We'll start a Joint Share Redemption Society in Messiah's name. What's his name anyway, this Jewish Messiah?

MENACHEM-JOSEF: God only knows!

JACKIE: Well, it doesn't matter. We'll call the society simply "The First Messiah Redemption Society." Five dollars a share, and when you have fifteen shares, you're redeemed.

MENACHEM-JOSEF *(Forgets himself for a moment):* From what?

JACKIE: The hell should I know. What difference does it make? Jews want someone to redeem them. Good. We'll redeem them. The main thing is, it'll make a buck. Ha! What do you say, Mr. Menachem-Josef? A good idea, or what?

MENACHEM-JOSEF: Yes. An excellent idea. Most of all, I like it because it's democratic. With us, there's no aristocrats, no fat cats. Pay your five dollars and you're redeemed. No second class redemption for the poor. They can be redeemed bit by bit.

JACKIE: You can be redeemed on the installment plan, as a special for the poor. Sort of a Third Class Redemption. How does this sound: you pay in fifty cents a day, in ten days you get a coupon. And in around 150 days, you're a redeemed man.

MENACHEM-JOSEF *(Thinks and thinks):* On the whole, the more I think about it, the more I like it. I like it better than the Spitter. I mean, the Spitter isn't bad either. Don't get me wrong. But he wants too much. If we make money on the Messiah, then later we can get the Spitter, too. But the thing is: where are we gonna get a Messiah?

JACKIE: I've been thinking about that. Where exactly can you get a Messiah? Hmmm . . . I have it! I have an uncle. He's a greenhorn—fresh off the boat. Been here for two weeks. From Galicia.[7] Still wears a big velvet hat and *peyes.*[8] It's like this: If we can persuade him . . . Hang on I'll just call him up. *(Into the telephone.)* Hello, Jackson 4031. Yes. Hello. Uncle! Uncle Simcha! This is

Jack. Yankel. Yes, Yaahnkel. Listen. Uncle. I have some business for you. Come over here. Take the train to 43rd Street. It's close by. But come right away. We'll wait. Ha! What? Well of course. You think it's free? Ok. fine. But don't delay; we're waiting *Goodbye. Goodbye. (Hangs up the telephone.)* He'll be here soon. You'll get a look at this bird. If this guy isn't the Messiah, I don't know who is. The main thing is, we can get him cheap because he's out of work. He's also sickly, so he can't do heavy work. And he can't spend too long on his feet. Also, he has a . . . you know, a . . . *(whispers in his ear)* hernia.

MENACHEM-JOSEF: It doesn't matter. On the contrary, it's even better. A Jewish Messiah should have a hernia. We should start thinking about a poster. Something like . . . It should just scream! With a portrait of Messiah and endorsements by rabbis and priests and all that stuff. The main thing, it should make a racket. *(The black phone rings.)* Who's speaking? Hah? The man from the furniture company? *(Angry. Disguises his voice.)* No. Menachem-Josef isn't in. Ha? What? Yes. He's out of town. Out of town? Ha? How long? For a year. *(Curt.)* Goodbye! *(Before he's hung up the little phone rings. He holds it and cradles it lovingly while saying goodbye into the other phone. Now he speaks gently and lyrically.)* Ha? Anna? How are you, my love? Yes. All's well. Jack and I are just setting up a great deal. Scoundrel Johnnie is going to look like a seven month runt next to us. Ha? No, I can't talk about it on the phone. Yes, my dearest. Thank you. What would I like to say to you? *What? Yes, of course I do . . . Good. Goodbye, sweetheart, goodbye. Goodbye. (The big phone rings again. He gives the phone a dirty look. The transformation from nice to nasty should*

be agile.) Ha? What? Who's speaking? The man from
the electric company? *(Suddenly very mild to Jack while
covering the mouthpiece.)* Do you know who that was?
That was Anna, the *Daytshke*[9] from the circus. *(To the
telephone.)* Ha? Mr. Menachem-Josef isn't here. *(Again
to* JACKIE, *gestures for him to take the phone.)*

JACKIE *(To the phone, like Menachem-Josef):* Ha? What? No.
Not here. Mr. Menachem-Josef is away. Where? Argentina.[10] *Yes. Goodbye!*

MENACHEM-JOSEF *(Irritated):* Money. Give them money.
Anything like money, but give them money. *(Different.
Practical. Takes a pencil in hand.)* So. That makes: 3,500
dollars a show, nine shows a week. We gross ... take away
rent ... and, uh ... and uh ... eighty-five ... 644 ... take-
away nineteen . . . leaves 18,000. Six eighths minus
thirty-one and a sixth, we have 921 times 811 ... carry
seven, take away sixteen ... leaves a total of ...

(Entrance of MESSIAH. *We hear a knock on the door.)*

JACKIE: That must be him, my uncle. We've gotta put on
our hats. *(To* MENACHEM-JOSEF.*)* Put on your hat. He's
a greenie, my uncle, fresh off the boat, and a fanatic. If
he sees us sitting around bareheaded he might not deal
with us at all. *(They put on hats.)*

(Enter MESSIAH.*)*

MESSIAH: *(An old, simple-minded Jew with a beard like a
broom, big curly peyes, wears a big velvet hat. A fanatical,
disapproving, laconic Jew who "suddenly finds himself in*

*the American wasteland." His Galitsianer accent should
be clear, not overdone. He substitutes "P" for "B".)*

JACKIE: *Sholem aleykhem*, uncle. *(Offers his hand.)* Sit down.

MESSIAH *(Sits)*: You needed me? *(Puffs on a pipe.)*

JACKIE: This is my boss, Mr. Menachem-Josef.

MENACHEM-JOSEF: *Sholem aleykhem. (Offers his hand, sizes
him up. Winks to* JACK, *"This is good.")*

MESSIAH: And . . . Well . . . ? What can I do for you?

JACKIE: *(Pokes* MENACHEM-JOSEF, *he should take things in
hand.)*

MENACHEM-JOSEF *(Getting excited):* It's like this Reb Uncle.
What was your name again?

MESSIAH: My name? They call me Simcha. Why?

JACKIE *(In uncle's ear):* Mr. Menachem-Josef is a great man.
He has a heart of gold.

MESSIAH *(Slow, reticent):* Mmh . . . Heart? Fine, but what do
you want from me?

MENACHEM-JOSEF *(Almost blurts something out, but quickly
stops himself):* All we want from you is just . . . . *(Different.)* Have you ever been in a theatre, Reb, uh, Reb Simcha?

MESSIAH: I was in a theatre, once. In Lemberg.[11] And so?

JACKIE: It doesn't matter. Mr. Menachem-Josef is just asking.

MESSIAH: Just asking?

MENACHEM-JOSEF *(Trying to draw him out):* And how did you like it, the theatre?

MESSIAH: How did I like? My daughter left me in the lobby. I looked in and saw it was dark. I didn't want to go in. Why should I sit in the dark? When the lights came on, I went in. What it's all about, I couldn't see. Ten cents an apple. fifteen cents for a bottle of soda water. The lights went out again, so I went back to the lobby and waited around. What would I do in the dark? Then I went in again. Still ten cents an apple, fifteen cents for soda water. So then I know. This is nothing with more nothing.

MENACHEM-JOSEF: *(All the while exploding in little bursts of suppressed laughter. Holds himself back. Scratches his head. Is lost in thought.)*

JACKIE *(Slaps him on the back):* Don't worry, uncle. With us, you'll learn a thing or two. And make a buck. And we'll give you an easy job, too.

MESSIAH: But heaven forbid, I won't have to work on Shabbos, will I?

JACKIE: What are you saying? That—Heaven forbid—we're not Jews?

MESSIAH: How would I know? In America, they say even the stones are treyf.

JACKIE: Don't believe it, uncle. In America there are a lot of pious Jews that pray and say the blessings and wash before eating and go to the bath house and even believe in the Messiah.

MESSIAH: *(Hears the word "Messiah" and lets out a long high-pitched sigh.)*

MENACHEM-JOSEF: It's like this. We'll give you thirty-five dollars a week to start.

MESSIAH *(Hesitant):* You'll give me thirty-five dollars a week? For what?

MENACHEM-JOSEF: For nothing. Just because I like your beard. *(Admires his beard.)* You have a very beautiful beard.

MESSIAH *(A little bit proud):* I have—praises be—a beautiful beard. Why not?

JACKIE: I'll say. A Jew with such a beard—*keyneynore*[12]—in America!

MENACHEM-JOSEF *(Proceeding as if on ice):* It's ... uh ... why shouldn't you, let's say ... so to speak, that is ... Is there a Messiah on Earth, do you believe?

MESSIAH *(Plainly):* What else? God forbid I shouldn't believe.

JACKIE *(Picks up the thread):* That's what I say. As soon as we all believe *(winks to* MENACHEM-JOSEF*)* then he must come. But why shouldn't he come a little sooner?

MENACHEM-JOSEF *(Blurts out):* And if he should come, why not directly to our firm? We've brought the greatest. Last year, we had Jack Dempsey and Kid McCoy.[13] Two years ago we had the guy who ate nails.

MESSIAH: Nails?

JACKIE: Nails, dear uncle, this big! *(Shows the length with his finger.)* He ate them.

MENACHEM-JOSEF: And the woman with three legs? Who brought her?

JACKIE: We did. We did.

MENACHEM-JOSEF: So. It's like this. Just sign this piece of paper . . . *(Writes something quickly on a piece of paper and hands it to him to sign.)*

JACKIE: Sign, uncle. Luck like this, you meet once in a hundred years. Just think, thirty-five dollars a week. For a greenie.

MENACHEM-JOSEF: It's a lot of money, but I'm doing it because of your nephew Jack. And because . . . I like your beard. You have a beautiful beard.

MESSIAH *(Proudly)*: We all have beautiful beards in our family. A livelihood, maybe not ...

JACKIE: You'll make a living too. As long as you're healthy. Sign.

MESSIAH: In Yiddish?

MENACHEM-JOSEF: In Yiddish. Of course in Yiddish. Do you think in America everything's *goyish*?

MESSIAH: I don't know. But I've already made a splotch. Should I blot it?

MENACHEM-JOSEF: No. It'll dry soon.

JACKIE: Leave it. It's good luck. *(Shakes his hand.)*

MENACHEM-JOSEF: Carry yourself like a man. You'll eat bread and butter with us.

JACKIE: Of course my uncle will do as he's told. What is he? Some kid who doesn't know about work?

MENACHEM-JOSEF: Later, when business is good, we'll give you, not thirty-five dollars a week, but forty-five dollars a week.

JACKIE: And maybe even fifty[14] *(To his uncle, softly.)* Do you know what that means? In your money, that's five-hundred Zlotys a week.[15] You'll be a big shot.

MESSIAH: Let me see. You give me thirty-five dollars a week, forty dollars a week, fifty dollars a week. But what I should do, you don't say.

JACKIE: You don't have to do anything, uncle. What should you do?

MESSIAH: Well, what should I do?

MENACHEM-JOSEF: Do? How shall I put it . . . Carry yourself like a man. Pious. Holy. Like a great rabbi. The main thing is the beard and the peyes. Don't—God forbid—cut them off.

MESSIAH: What are you saying? *(Grabs his beard and peyes as if to shield them from harm.)* Heaven forbid! *(Smiles graciously.)* It's for the beard and peyes you're paying me thirty-five dollars a week?

JACKIE: What do you think, uncle? In America, do we know how to value *Yiddishkeit*, or what?

MESSIAH: Of course, it sounds wonderful. May God smile on you. Well then, I'll go home.

MENACHEM-JOSEF: Wait. We need to photograph you.

MESSIAH: What for?

JACKIE: Don't worry, uncle, we need this for . . . business.

MESSIAH: What business?

MENACHEM-JOSEF: We need to show the world that there are still real Jews in America.

JACKIE: Do it, uncle. What are worrying about? Moishe Montefiore[16] had his picture taken, and you, not?

MESSIAH: I dunno. Fine. *(Gives himself over.)*

JACKIE *(Calls into the next room): Hey Jim*! Bring out the camera!

(Enter JIM.*)*

JIM *(An Irishman with a red face. Chews and spits continually. Sleeves rolled up, white cap with the logo of a flour company, "Hekersey Flour"[17] that the company gives away free for advertising. He brings out the camera):* Who?

JACKIE: That guy.

JIM: Full length or just the head? *(Spits.)*

JACKIE *(To* MENACHEM-JOSEF*):* What do you think? I think just the head is good.

MENACHEM-JOSEF *(Joking):* Just the head is already too much. If you could just take the beard.

MESSIAH *(Grabs his beard):* What are you saying?

JACKIE: Don't be scared, uncle. Mr. Menachem-Josef just means take a picture of the beard.

MESSIAH: I see! I thought you meant . . .

(Scene: The photographer, a bit of a joker, sets up the camera like a machine-gun. MESSIAH *keeps backing away. Jim goes after him with the camera. They keep circling in one direction. Finally goes under the black cloth and waves his hands.)*

JIM: Stop moving.

MESSIAH *(To* JACK*):* I don't like this. Why's this *goy* hiding his face? Tell him not to hurt me.

JACKIE: Don't be afraid, uncle. He won't hurt you.

MESSIAH: If he's not going to hurt me, why's he hiding?

JACKIE: He has to.

MESSIAH *(Gives in):* Well, so be it. If he must, he must. It won't hurt, will it Yankel?

JACKIE: It won't hurt, uncle. Why should it hurt?

MESSIAH: How should I know? This is America.

JIM *(Loads the camera, frightening* MESSIAH*):* Smile a little, please.

MESSIAH: Why should I smile? *(To* JACK*)* Do I have to smile, Yankel?

JACKIE: You have to, uncle.

MESSIAH: So be it. You gotta do what you gotta do. *(Weakly)* Wait a minute. Get me some water. I don't feel good.

JIM: *(Brings him water. He drinks like one about to faint.)*

JIM *(Impatiently):* So. Smile! *(Angrily)* Smile already, God-dammit!

MESSIAH: *(Smiles like someone who's had his throat cut. There's a pop from the flash, which frightens him. He falls off his chair.)*

JIM: *(Leaves smiling. Looks at* MESSIAH *like a wild man.)*

MESSIAH *(Groans):* It's not so easy to earn a little bread.

Jack: *(Helps him.)*

MESSIAH: Mhh . . . . Thank God it's over. Can I go now?

(All the while, MENACHEM-JOSEF *has been talking with* JACK.*)*

MENACHEM-JOSEF *(Smoking a cigar):* To tell you the truth, I'd rather have you start right away. *(To* JACK.*)* We have to work the press. We have to call the reporters, get them over here at once. *(Remembers.)* We've got to let the editors know before they go to press. Maybe we can break the story today. *(To* JACK.*)* Meanwhile, take this bird of yours to the next room.

JACKIE *(To* MESSIAH*):* Come, uncle, we'll go in here for a bit.

MESSIAH: What for?

JACKIE: We have to, uncle, we have to.

MESSIAH: Well. You gotta do what you've gotta do. *(JACK and* MESSIAH *off.)*

(Before they've quite left the room, MENACHEM-JOSEF *falls to dialing the telephone, hot and heavy.)*

MENACHEM-JOSEF: *Hello. Hello.* The Yellow News? It's me, Menachem-Josef. A tremendous sensation. Messiah. Yes. Messiah. Offering redemption in three classes. Yes. Redemption in three classes. Shabbos and Sunday matinees. Yes. For people of all walks of life. Ha? Yes, exclusive with our firm. Yes. With a big headline. Does he redeem Social Democrats? Of course! He's a Social Democrat himself. You'll get this out quick? In today's paper? Good. Send your reporter right over. Thanks. *Goodbye. (Hangs up the telephone and picks it back up immediately.)* The Black News? *Yes*, me. A tremendous sensation . . . Messiah . . . Yes, exclusively with us. Does he redeem Zionists, too? Of course! He's a Zionist himself. Yeh. Five dollars a share. Yes, installment plan, too . . . . But it's better to buy all the shares at once. You see. It'll come out today? And send your reporter. Yes, it'll make a racket. Goodbye. *(Puts down the phone, picks it up again.) Hello, hello*? The Grey News? Yes. Menachem-Josef speaking. A tremendous sensation. Messiah. Exclusively with our firm. Does he redeem Labour Zionists?[18] Of course! He's a Labour Zionist himself. See it goes into today's paper. With a big headline, "Messiah In America", yes? Good. Thanks. Yes . . . Send your reporter right away. *(He puts down the phone, exhausted, wipes away sweat. Remembers.)* Oh yeah, I've gotta dictate notices and announcements for the press. Completely forgot. *(Calls into the door, left, that* JIM *came out of earlier.)* Flossie!

(Enter FLOSSIE.*)*

FLOSSIE *(A young girl with a pretty, stupid face, dressed in a very short skirt with silk stockings. Heavy makeup, red lipstick, paper cuffs on a neat green silk blouse, she has a pencil stuck in her bottle-blonde hair. Speaks very coolly and is constantly aware of being a member of the fairer sex, and that her boss isn't indifferent to her. Holds a pencil and steno pad in her hand):* Yes!

MENACHEM-JOSEF *(Smitten like a kitten):* Sit by me Flossie, right here, I want to dictate to you. *(He wants to give her a feel.)*

FLOSSIE *(Pretending she doesn't want to):* Dictate! But with your mouth. I don't like it.

MENACHEM-JOSEF: That's what they all say.

FLOSSIE: I'm not "all". I'm me.

MENACHEM-JOSEF *(Suddenly loses romantic interest. Becomes all business):* It's like this. Figure like so. *(Takes a pencil and figures.)* So . . . ten newspapers . . . eight weeklies . . . not counting posters and handbills. All told . . . *(To* FLOSSIE, *who's waiting with a sharp pencil. All the while, she's been sharpening it in the little machine attached to the table.)* Take dictation, dear, only don't make any mistakes.

FLOSSIE *(Annoyed):* So. Let's hear already.

MENACHEM-JOSEF *(Dictates with his hand over his eyes like someone who is choosing his thoughts precisely):* Messiah In America! Heading. Exclamation mark. The firm Menachem-Josef and company, comma, has brought the Messiah. Dash. Exclusively for the redemption of the Jewish people, comma, of the Exile. For all classes and walks of life, colon. For five dollars a share. *(Differently.)* Did you write five dollars a share? Erase it, Flossie, dear. Write: For all classes and all walks of life, five dollars for the entire redemption—exclamation mark! The Messiah moment—hyphen—is the greatest—underlined—in our history, semicolon. Did you write "history" yet? Erase, Flossie, dear. Write of the tragic history of—write di-a-spora, di-a-spora, but without mistakes. You always write di-a-spora with mistakes.

FLOSSIE *(Moves closer, flirtatiously):* Is that all, Mr. Menachem-Josef?

MENACHEM-JOSEF: *(Gets up. Puts on his glasses. Puts his arm around her, ostensibly to read the notice in her hand. She doesn't struggle. He bends to kiss her. There's a knock on the door.)*

(Exit FLOSSIE.*)*

MENACHEM-JOSEF *(Sits back in his chair looking very much the boss):* Who's there?

VOICES: *(Sung.)*
Yellow.
Black.
Grey.

MENACHEM-JOSEF: Enter!
(Enter GREY, BLACK, YELLOW. GREY *is dressed in grey, which is a little like blue and a little like white.* BLACK, *like a religious functionary is dressed entirely in black, and wears a yarmulke.* YELLOW *is fat and wears a yellow costume and a top hat which is painted to look like a ten-storey building, the symbol of the New York yellow press, Forverts.)*

ALL THREE *(In operatic chorus):*
We raise our hands to heaven *(they do so)* and pray
That we make Jewish sorrow pay.
We believe in the Holy Yiddish Word.
We believe in God and Messiah, his Vassal.
Give us a dollar and there'll be no hassle.
We uphold ancient market ways:
See a rich man, sing his praise.

(From here on the shtick unfolds like an operetta with all sorts of precious gestures and bombast. Sung if possible or recitative.)

MENACHEM-JOSEF: Please sit down, it must be wearing,
You must be tired from all that swearing.

ALL THREE: *(In chorus.)*
One can never tire to do
The work of the eternal Jew.

Our will will not die
To raise the flag high
Of our past so glorious,
King David victorious.
David our eternal king!
David our eternal king!

MENACHEM-JOSEF *(With his hand on his heart, sings):*
It gives me joy, my fellow Jews
To know the joy this gives to you:
The great deed that we do today

ALL THREE *(In chorus):* Long live Messiah! Hooray! Hooray!

MENACHEM-JOSEF: Now Messiah, boys, he ain't no fool
To make a buck's his golden rule.
And since business is holy, like the God of the Wise,
Messiah, himself, will be our merchandise.

ALL THREE: Long live the Jew as he follows his ways
And chases a living the rest of his days.

MENACHEM-JOSEF: And so, my friends, set.
I see you're working up a sweat.

*(*YELLOW, GREY, BLACK *sit all in a row like clowns.)*

MENACHEM-JOSEF:
Our daily press is a thing of great might,
Persuading all that day is night.
And so, I ask you, dear gentlemen,
By word and by deeds to further my ends.

ALL THREE:
  We'll be helpful, helpful, helpful.
  Helpful are we,
  Endlessly.

MENACHEM-JOSEF:
  Thank you. Thank you. Thank you, so.
  You may go.
  But do not waiver
  To write in your paper
  That I am the savior
  Of all Israel
  Who suffer under the Cross.

ALL THREE IN CHORUS: *(Again, raise their hands, Exit. On the way out.)*
  You can count on us to take dictation
  And tell it to the nation.

  (All three exit with their hands in the air.)

  (Enter MESSIAH, *after him,* JACK.*)*

MESSIAH *(To* JACK*):* Well, fine. What you've gotta do, you've gotta do.

JACKIE *(Slaps him on the shoulder):* Now you're talking like a man, uncle.

MESSIAH *(A foolish smile. Remembers):* What did you say I should say if people ask me something? Yankel?

JACKIE: I said if they ask something just weasel out of it. Say, "I have spoken. . . ." You coulda spoke yes, you coulda spoke no, according to what you want. Understand?

MESSIAH *(As he's been taught):* I have spoken. . .

(We hear a cry from the street. "M—e—s—s—i—a—h!" "Extra!" "Messiah In America!" "Hey — Extra!" followed by the murmur of the crowd outside the door and a cry of Mess—i—ah!)

MENACHEM-JOSEF *(Looks out the window and listens):* The papers are already out with the story. The crowd is headed this way, fast and furious. *(To* JACK.*)* Hide him.

JACKIE *(To* MESSIAH*):* Come, uncle, the crowd mustn't see you. It's still too early. The time is not yet come. Let 'em buy tickets first . . . What do you say, uncle?

MESSIAH *(As he's been taught):* I have spoken . . . *(This could mean, I have spoken yes or I have spoken no . . .)*

(Enter the Crowd.)

FIRST: Where's The Messiah?

SECOND: We've come for The Messiah.

THIRD: We want to see him with our own eyes.

MENACHEM-JOSEF *(Like a prophet):* The time is not yet come, Jews.

First: Give us Messiah.

Second: We can't wait any longer.

Third: We've waited too long.

First: Messiah!

Second: Redimmer.

First: Don't say "Redimmer". Say "Redeemer".

Second: What's the difference? Redimmer. Redeemer. As long as he redims.

First: He doesn't redim. He redeems.

Second: What's the difference? Redims. Redeems. As long as he's a Redimmer.

Third: Messiah! Messiah!

Menachem-Josef: Messiah is over there. *(Points.)* But you may not see him, for the time is not yet come.
(A great noise from the Crowd, which pushes forward. All gather around the door where Messiah *is secreted with* Jack. *Some carry lit candles, Others carry palm fronds. They sing as in the play* Sabbetai Zevi.[19] *Among the Crowd, women , cripples, blind men, beggars.)*

Crowd: Hosanna! For Thy sake, our God! For Thy sake, our God. Hosanna! *(Singing is very eloquent. The door opens and all look in.* Messiah *comes out,* Jack *with him.)*

SHRIEKING: Messiah! Messiah!
(They gather around him, dance around him in great en-thusiasm.)

MESSIAH: Jews. *(It goes quiet.)*

VOICES: Shhhhhhhh! Messiah wants to say something. *(Grows very quiet.)*

FIRST: He's opening his mouth!

SECOND: He's going to speak!

THIRD: Shhhhhhhhh . . . . . !

MESSIAH: I want to tell the truth, Jews. I am a simple Jew . . . A sick man . . . I need to make a living. *(Apparently wants to confess that he's been dragged into a sham.)*

JACKIE: All Messiahs are poor.

MENACHEM-JOSEF: As it is written: "He shall be a poor man."

CROWD: Mess—i—ah! Mess—i—ah! Messiah of the poor and downtrodden!

MESSIAH *(Wants to say something, but* JACK *and* MEN-ACHEM-JOSEF *stand on either side of him, keeping him in check):* Jews . . .

MENACHEM-JOSEF: Jews! Messiah is poor and hungry. Why do you hold back?

JACKIE: I'll give the first fifty dollars. *(Takes out a banknote and lays it on the table.)* Who will give next?

MENACHEM-JOSEF: I'll give my diamond pin. And my ring. *(Takes it off and lays this treasure on the table.)*

MESSIAH *(Almost moved to tears):* Jews. No ... This ... I have sp...

JACKIE *(Pushes aside the last words):* It's not enough, Jews. Give what you can. Give more. Why do you hold back? Jews ... Stubborn mules!

(The Crowd removes their watches, earrings treasures of all sorts, silk scarfs — they pile them up on the table, a whole mountain of silver, gold, silk, diamonds, pearls, etc.)

MESSIAH: Jews! ... I have ...

MENACHEM-JOSEF: Jews! Give more. Don't hold back. It's not enough. *(Jews—men and women—drag out wallets, purses, and give away their last dollar.)*

(Enter HUNCHBACK.)

HUNCHBACK *(Draws near):* I am a poor cripple. I have no money, no treasure. I have only an amulet with a pearl that my mother, may she rest in peace, gave me to protect me from poverty. *(He removes from his sunken chest a dirty wallet and unwraps from its cloth a single pearl on a filthy string and brings it to* MESSIAH *himself.)* Take this, Messiah, Holy One, and redeem us.

VOICES: Deliver us! We can't wait any longer.
— Messiah! — Messiah!
Ben David. . . . Redeemer!
Hosanna! For Thy sake, our God! For Thy sake, our God! Hosanna!

MESSIAH *(Stands with the pearl in his hand):* Jews, I can not . . . I am not . . . *(Grimaces several times as if about to fall. Falls.)*

CROWD: He's fallen! Our Messiah!
— Messiah! Messiah!
— The time is not yet come.

(A great silent sadness reigns. All gather round the fallen MESSIAH *and hang their heads, lost and broken. A quiet lament from the crowd.)*

CROWD: Our king. Our Messiah.

(All the while MENACHEM-JOSEF *and* JACKIE BLUFFER *edge closer to the footlights. The latter holds a bag full of gold and silver that he's swiped. He jingles the bag of loot.)*

JACKIE: A shame, my greenie uncle. Poor thing. But it's not our fault. Business is business.

MENACHEM-JOSEF: Not for nothing is it written that Messiah will come riding an ass. He came riding a whole bunch of asses.

JACKIE: Without asses, there's no Messiah. (*Differently.*) Now I can buy a new automobile. A good one.

MENACHEM-JOSEF: And I can take my little *Daytsh* cutie to Florida. *(Plays with the lone pearl on the dirty string.)*

(*The Crowd's wailing becomes stronger, louder. Especially* HUNCHBACK, *who gave the last pearl.*)

Curtain.

Act II

Act II

Scene One

A Golden Calf is brought on stage. A song is sung by an assortment of bourgeois folk.

The sun shines on high and the swallow flies freely
But our wonderful Calf is all that is holy.

We bow to you, our prayers are yours,
Oh Calf, please open Heaven's doors.

(All bow in dance.)

Gold. Give us Gold. Give us more.
Open up the Golden Door.

Let Golden Rain come down in sheets,
Let Golden Tiles pave our streets.

Oh lovely idol, Idol of Gold,
For you we've sold off treasures untold.

Oh you, our God.
Our only God.
Almighty God.

(Bow again.)

Gold! Give us Gold!
Gold Gold Gold.
Yellow Gold.
Lovely round coins, blood-red Gold.

Oh Gold!
Give us Gold.

Oh Idol of Gold, we serve only you.
We bow only to you, we pray only to you.

Oh Gold.
Give us Gold.

(Dancers exit with Calf, which is on wheels.)

Scene Two

The stage is arranged to give an ever-changing impression of being backstage and onstage. The characters are shown getting into their costume. A turn of folding doors and the stage becomes a street in Coney Island. An exhibit hall. Posters and advertisements for the sideshow. Outside, we hear the pounding racket of a band.

SCOUNDREL JOHNNIE *(Later* ZIP*):* Where's the Indian? The Indian! Where is he? Hey! Flossie! This Indian of ours, have you seen him anywhere? We have to open already.

FLOSSIE: The Indian isn't coming in today.

SCOUNDREL JOHNNIE: How come?

FLOSSIE: He telephoned. It's his father's *yortsayt.*[20] He's gotta go to synagogue and say Kaddish.

SCOUNDREL JOHNNIE: That's what you get when you hire *landslayt.*[21] *(Irritated.)* Would it have killed me to hire a German or a Pole? But no, I had to go hire a Jew. A Jew for an Indian. I'm an idiot.

FLOSSIE: Don't get angry Mr. Zipkin. He's no big deal anyway. An Indian? Some freak! Believe me, Mr. Zipkin, my boyfriend, the Bearded Lady is a bigger attraction than ten Indians.

SCOUNDREL JOHNNIE: Your boyfriend! Your boyfriend, the Bearded Lady! All we ever hear is your boyfriend. Everybody's got something, she's got a boyfriend, the Bearded Lady. *(Ambiguously.)* Are you really saving yourself for him, Flossie, dear? *(Calls out.)* Noise! Noise! Make a little noise! *(We hear a racket from the band.)*

FLOSSIE *(With a little smile. Twirls her hair. Pops her bubble-gum):* There's nothing left to save.

SCOUNDREL JOHNNIE: You don't say! Who's the lucky fellow?

FLOSSIE *(Easily):* That guy from Kovno[22] stole my honour. Didn't you know?

SCOUNDREL JOHNNIE: Fine, fine. Nothing to speak of. That's what I get for giving you a job. With me, you play. With others, you sleep.

FLOSSIE *(Relaxed):* S'allright, I'll get even with him, with that Kovno *Daytsh*. He'll get his. I'm suing him for thirty thousand dollars damages for breaking my heart. His only chance is to run off somewhere I can't find him. The bastard.

SCOUNDREL JOHNNIE: You've got a good head on you for business, Flossie. *(Forgets.)* So .... Where's that damned Indian? I'm not hiring any more Jews in my business. I'll tell you what. Jews. I'm not having any Jews work here. Not as Turks, not as Indians, not as Chinese. *(Looks at his watch.)* I'm afraid we'll have to open with you, Flossie. Come. Get on the broom. It's time to open. Hot today. Yecch. *(Wipes sweat.)*

FLOSSIE: Where's the broom?

SCOUNDREL JOHNNIE: *(Fastens her to the broom. She lies down horizontally. It's done by fastening a hook which attaches to a back-brace under her dress. The hook is hidden in the broad end of the broom. With a turn of the wings, the crowd comes into view. The music pounds. The ticket seller pulls tickets off a roll. He waves his hands wildly urging the crowd in from outside.)*

BARKER *(CHARLIE): Big Show! Big Show. Come on in. Biggest Show on di Island. (Through a megaphone.)* The Greatest Show in Coney Island . . . The Greatest Show in Coney Island. Only ten cents. Ten! Ten! Cents! Only ten cents. One *dime. Two nickels! Ladies and Gentlemen. Big Show, Big Show! Show Show Show. Big-Big-Big.*

(Pause.)

Step right up, step right up! The show is about to begin. Do you see the lady? She floats in mid air. *(Passes his hand under her body.)* By magic. Black magic. Black as night. Magic. Magic. Lady. Lady. Night. Night. Floats. Floats. Cock-a-doodle-do. Cock-a-doodle-do. Come on in! Come on in! Everybody in. Ten cents. Ten cents. Only ten little pennies. One dime! The Greatest and the Best that the world has to offer for ten cents. For the price of a loaf of bread.Come on in. Come on in. Everybody in. *(Waves his hands as if to draw them in by magic.)*

(On the left a missionary speaks in gross vulgar language. He's a little drunk and stammers a bit.)

MISSIONARY: Jesus will save you! He set me on my feet. *(Almost falls.)* He'll put you, put you on your feet. Believe in Jesus. I say whoever doesn't believe in Jesus Christ is a rat bastard and a lousy snot. You don't go to church except on Sundays. Sometimes not even then. When you croak what do you think's going to become of you? You don't know? *Alright*, I'll tell you. When you come to the Gates of Paradise, Jesus is going to give you a smack in the face. "*No sir*" is what he'll say. "Boys, I haven't prepared a place in Paradise for you. *Nosiree*." *(Someone rushes at him.)* You'll want to fight. Oh, *alright*! Sons of bitches. Jesus can fight, too. Oh, yes! Jesus can bloody all your faces—oh yes! As it is written—when Jesus came and saw you were dragging around a woman of the streets—a whore—he cried out "Stop," Oh, yes! They were afraid and set the woman loose. *Ladies and gentlemen* Jesus Christ saved me. Oh yes! *(Hiccups.)* He saved *(Hiccups.)* me.

BARKER *(To* MISSIONARY*):* Stop all this bother with Jesus. You're interfering with business.

MISSIONARY: God is the best business. *(Hiccups.)*

BARKER: *Ladies and gentlemen*, I ask you, is it fair to ruin our business? Sunday of all days? The best day in Coney Island? I ask you, which would you rather, business or religion?

CROWD: Business, business, business!

PART OF THE CROWD *(To* MISSIONARY*):* Pipe down! Pipe down!

ANOTHER PART: The Missionary's right. Religion's better than business.

ANOTHER: God is God and business is business.

ANOTHER: Business is greater than God.

(There's a tussle, first between Missionary and Barker and then among the crowd. The drunken Missionary has to give way.)

MISSIONARY: Jew! Sheeny!

BARKER: Your God's a Jew too, a sheeny.

MISSIONARY: My God isn't a Jew. He's an Israelite. *(Laughter.)*

BARKER: Your God was a Jew. Not an Israelite. He was a sheeny.

MISSIONARY: You're a Jew. You're a sheeny. All Jews are *sonofabitches*. We should strangle you like mice, we oughta, lousy Jews. You wait. I'll get even, God damn you.

BARKER *(Keeps pushing him):* Go on! Out of there! Before I plant one on your snout.

MISSIONARY: Who? Me?

BARKER: You! You!

MISSIONARY: You're going to give me one in the snout?

BARKER: I'm going to give you one in the snout.

MISSIONARY: Who? You?

BARKER: Yes. Me.

MISSIONARY *(Differently, half drunk):* Allright. If that's how it is, I'll go away.

(Exit Missionary.)

Scene Three

The Side Show in Coney Island

Canvas tent. The ground is covered with sawdust. Cages with freaks. Above each is a plaque with his characteristics and portrait. The Barker leads a group of people from one place to another. Explains the marvels.

FAKIR: *(Fire-eater, sword-swallower, dressed in a uniform. Does tricks with cards. Finally sells Magic Horseradish for fifty cents a bottle.)*

ANOTHER: *(Performs guessing game tricks. Blindfolded, he works in cahoots with his questioner. That guy shows him, for example, a pen knife and says,* "Ikh halt in hent a meserl—Tell di gentlemen vat I hev in my hend." *The rest should be said quickly,* "Ikh halt in hent a meserl" *[in Yiddish] The second part is said clearly in English so the crowd doesn't catch on.)*

SOAP-SELLER: *(With suds on his head and hands)* Soap! Soap! Wonder Soap! *(Pours water on his own head and makes suds.)* This is the best soap in the world. The only soap that doesn't change its colour. All other American soaps change their colour like our politicians. But not my soap. All those who suffer from diabetes, from pneumonia, chorditis, tuberculosis, from cancer, from milk-fever, from appendicitis you'll be cured with just this very soap! Buy my soap and you'll be beautiful as the sun, wise as the day, strong as Samson the Mighty, rich as Croesus. That's a fact! *(He is surrounded by old ladies. On to the other freaks.)*

BARKER: This is Atabandu the Hindu, the greatest wonder of the century. He swallows fire the way Italians swallow noodles. The way Jews swallow matzo. The way Russians swallow *kapusta*.[20] Mr. Atabandu, please.

HINDU *(Performs tricks. Then speaks gibberish): Giveri, durandar, hokum, dilibanda, Africa.*

SOMEONE FROM THE CROWD: You're an Indian?

HINDU: *(Nods his head, yes.)*

ANOTHER: Not a Litvak?

HINDU: *(Shakes his head, no.)*

ANOTHER: Do you speak Yiddish?

HINDU: *(Shakes his head, no.)*

ANOTHER: And you've never been to Minsk?

HINDU *(Overjoyed):* Minsk? Are you a Minsker? Would you believe it...?
(Catches himself. Goes back to speaking gibberish. Laughter from the crowd.)

HALF-MAN, HALF-WOMAN: *(Behind a curtain. Special Attraction. Speaks a few words in a hoarse voice. Doesn't look at anybody. Shows her chest: the short, flat breast and the round one.)*

BARKER: *Ladies and Gentlemen!* You now stand before one of the greatest wonders of medical science: Nature has, so to speak, divided her in half and given her both sexes in the same body. *(Joking.)* So she could practically marry herself. But joking aside, Madam Olgarina sells a picture of her naked body. This is only available to medical students. Whoever among this distinguished crowd is a medical student can come forward to buy. Only fifty cents. And you don't need a diploma. You only need to tell us you're a medical student. We'll believe you. *(Many people surge forward)* We don't believe that in such a fine audience as we see here before us today, you could find anyone who would not tell the truth. *(Pause.)* And now we come to the greatest wonder of the century, The Bearded Lady, Mrs. Meyer. *(Leads the crowd.)* The Lady herself would like to say a few words, but sadly, she's caught a cold and cannot speak today. Mrs. Meyer was born in North Dakota of Spanish parents. Her father was a mathematics teacher in Barcelona. Her mother was a famous dancer in Argentina. Mrs. Meyer began growing a beard when she was sixteen years old. Instead of spending money to get rid of the hair on her face, as many women do these days, she let her beard grow. And now she has a beard that many men might envy. Mrs. Meyer speaks several languages, among them Scandinavian and Russian. Unfortunately she has a cold today. Ladies and gentlemen, buy postcards with her photograph, only ten cents apiece.

(She offers cards for sale.)

BARKER: And now, friends, we have the famous, the greatest All-American game, called, as you know, "*Hit the Nigger.*"[24] Hit the *Nigger*, it's called. Our show was the first to introduce the new sport of throwing balls at a *Nigger*. Because our show is a progressive circus, always at the forefront of popular taste. Ladies and gentlemen, the *Nigger* on show here today is fresh out of prison where he languished fifteen years for defiling a woman. *(The* NIGGER *sticks out his tongue and says)* Bah! *(We don't know if he's laughing or confirming.)* As you all know, *Niggers* are habitual rapists, thieves and bandits. It's well known that in the Southern States of our land, they shoot *niggers* like dogs. In the South they have segregated trolleys and segregated buses for them. I hope the time is not far off when our glorious North will follow their example and establish segregated seating for blacks. *(Short pause.)* Buy balls to throw at the *Nigger*. Five cents a ball, ten balls for forty-five cents. Hit the *Nigger. (Demonstrates.)* Aim straight for the head. Whoever hits the *Nigger* in the head wins a prize: a lovely little Bible with a leather cover and gold embossing. Hit the *Nigger. (Smiles. Holds up two tickets. Offers them.) Who wants to hit a Nigger? Step right up, gentlemen, there's no time to waste. (Produces balls and the game is on. They throw balls. The* NIGGER *grimaces comically. When someone hits him he says in Yiddish,* "'kh'hob dikh in dr'erd."* [25] A cry goes up. "Hit the Jew. Hit him. He's a fake!")*

BARKER: And now, my friends, we stand before the very greatest wonder of our age. The Ossified Man. "Ossified" means he's turned to stone! Mr. Williams case is one seldom seen in medicine. His entire body is hardened like flint. Try touching his head. His feet will jump. Try it. Go ahead. Don't be afraid. This is no hoax. Mr. Williams has certificates from doctors that he can at most live another six months before his heart turns to stone. Then he's through! Mr. Williams himself would like to say a few words.

WILLIAMS *(Lies horizontally, on display. Smokes a cigarette on a toothpick):* Ladies and gentlemen. As you can see from the testimonies that hang over my platform, little by little, my body is turning to stone. *(Proudly)* Today, I am the only man in America, I can say, in the entire world, who suffers from this disease. I can live at most six months before it invades my heart. Buy my postcards. Fifteen cents apiece, fifteen cents apiece.

FROM THE CROWD: Why fifteen cents? With everyone else it's ten and with you it's fifteen.

WILLIAMS *(Calmly):* My dear gentleman. You forget that I am the only case in all of medical science and that I can live at most six more months. Fifteen cents is no big deal. Fifteen cents apiece. Fifteen cents apiece. *(Mechanically)* Postcards! Postcards. Who wants postcards?

(Crowd gives way.)

BARKER: And now, *Ladies and gentlemen*, we stand before

the greatest wonder of the century. Lady Evelyn Nesbit Simpson.[26] This is the famous so-called "Hammer Murderess". She let her husband have it over the head with a hammer and killed him. For a long time, this was the greatest sensation in the land, as you know. Not because the lady killed her husband, but the racy way she killed him, and the incident that lead up to it. As you all know, the court found Lady Evelyn Nesbit Simpson not guilty and released her. Now the distinguished lady Evelyn Nesbit Simpson will tell you all the details of how she killed her husband with a hammer. (*To her.*) *Please*, Mrs. Evelyn Nesbit!

LADY NESBIT (*Coolly filing her nails*): *Ladies and gentlemen*, I killed my husband on the night of February twenty-ninth. It was at 2:05 am. I had just come home from the theatre. He lay in bed, asleep. But he was not sleeping quietly as usual—he was snoring. He had a cold. It got on my nerves, so I looked for the revolver to shoot him, but I couldn't find it. All the while, I had a headache. So I went into the bathroom and rubbed eau de Cologne on my temples. As I was leaving the bathroom, I suddenly noticed an iron hammer. The man who fixed the plumbing had left it behind. I picked up the hammer and went straight to the bedroom. I heard him still snoring away. I hit him in the head with the hammer. That shut him up. He gave a jerk, let out a cry, and that was it. The whole pillow was spattered. My husband was a gentleman and a good Christian. We were married for over nine years. He was born in North Dakota and was a businessman. I too am a good Christian and go to church every day. Here is the hammer I killed him with. (*Shows the hammer.*) Buy my postcards.

Twenty cents apiece. Twenty cents apiece. *Ladies and gentlemen.* With a picture of the hammer. Thank you. *(They buy.)*

BARKER *(Stands next to the Fat Lady's booth): Ladies and gentlemen,* you now stand before the greatest wonder in the world, Miss Madison, the world's fattest lady. She weighs 380 pounds. Miss Madison is a cultivated woman and one hundred percent American. Her ancestors came to America aboard the Mayflower. Miss Madison herself belongs to the very distinguished woman's club, The Daughters of the American Revolution,[27] which is so dedicated to remembering our heroic soldiers who have lost one or more legs in the last war. Miss Madison specializes in left legs. She knows by heart the names and addresses of all the veterans of the European war who have only left legs. Unfortunately, the lady cannot experience the joys of family life because her belly to too large. But aside from that, she's completely normal, sexually and otherwise. She is a thoroughly normal American girl. *Ladies and gentlemen,* if anyone among you wishes to ask Miss Madison a question, you may do so. Miss Madison will answer any question on diet, religion or pinochle. Miss Madison will also gladly recite the names of all 9896 American soldiers, veterans of the World War who have only left legs. Please, Miss Madison.

MISS MADISON *(Speaking from memory):* Jim Dublin, 1263 Madison Ave, New York; Estery Hudson, 1229 Gotham Street, Washington; Albert Rush Nomberg, 1389 Bay Parkway, Chicago; William Anderson Midmorn, 1480 Blue Island Avenue, Detroit; John L. Piccard, 619 Lincoln Boulevard, San Francisco; Boris Esterson, 19 Hop Street, Saint Louis; Victor Hasbrook, Gandy Road, Boston *(Sees the crowd losing interest)* Buy my post-cards. Only ten cents apiece. *(While the crowd is standing around The Fat Lady, the spotlight turns to "ZIP".)*

ZIP *(Quietly)*: You've got to give them more humour, Charlie. Your oration, your talk is too dry.

CHARLIE *(Quietly):* I'm doing everything I can to hold them, Mr. Zipkin.

ZIP: Yes, but the visitors are getting bored. We can't let them get bored. Remember the rule, Charlie. Our American audience will swallow anything, as long as you amuse them. Cut a slice off their pockets as long as you tickle them with the same scissors you used to cut their pockets. Menachem-Josef, the bastard, understands this. And P.T. Barnum, too. That's how they cleaned up. *(Differently)* I hear that Menachem-Josef is making a pile of money with his Messiah. I hear . . .

BARKER: That's what they say. Yesterday I read that he bought a section of the cemetery in Brooklyn and offered a deal to bury the dead standing. The plots are smaller, so you can bury them cheap. The New York Yiddish-English press—they're praising him to the skies. They call him a philanthropist. "The father of the poor," they're calling him. The Times says the news will bring real relief to paupers who've put off dying because they can't afford to get themselves buried. Now they can go ahead and die. For sixty-five dollars, even a poor man can afford to be dead. That's what The Times says. Even if the dead have to stay on their feet all the time. It's not a problem. Nowhere is it written that a poor man must spend all the days of his death stretched out like an aristocrat. It's perfectly normal, it won't bother the paupers a bit if they stand. After all, they didn't get to sit down so much in life, either. He's going to make a fortune, our Menachem-Josef.

ZIP: He's like a pig's snout. He swallows everything up. Well, *s'allright.* I'll outdo him. *Oh, yes*. It's true, he's got a good head on him, our little Menachem-Josef. But Zip's head hasn't dried up either. Never mind. Thanks to God, Zip's still got a head on his shoulders.

Barker *(Flatteringly):* I think you've got more brains than Menachem-Josef. That guy's just had more luck.

ZIP *(Angry):* Luck, shmuck! I've got luck, too. Luck? You don't need luck. Smarts, that's what you need. *(Smacks his forehead.)* Luck, he says! Well he's not walking around wearing a golden halo just yet. With his lousy one or two million dollars. I laugh at him. Such a rich man. Well, like him, I'm ready for it at any time. Menachem-Josef, he says.

BARKER: That's not what I'm saying, I was just trying to say . . . . Look They're leaving already.

ZIP: *(Changes his costume before our eyes. Slips into a fuzzy yellow costume and puts on an outrageous comic wig. A bald cap with a bonnet on top. He picks up a fiddle and takes on the look of an imbecile with his lip hanging down. Smiles idiotically and plays the fiddle.)*

BARKER *(Breezily. Holds a long pose. Coughs):* Ladies and gentlemen. You now stand before the GGGGRRR-REEEAAATTTEEESSSTTT wonder in the whole world and of all time. It's "Zip". Who is that? Zip is a riddle that no man can understand. To this very day, science has not been able to determine Zip's race, nation or sex. Zip is raceless and sexless, without conscience or principles, un-wived, un-manned, fatherless, motherless, thoughtless and of no party. In short, he is the biggest nothing in the whole world. Zip speaks his own language. But even the greatest linguists cannot ascertain what sort of language it is. It's not Hindustani, it's not Spanish. It's not Yiddish. It's not Turkish. It's not Tatar. *(In the tone of a Yiddish Talmudic dispute, for comic effect.)* And it's also not not-Yiddish, and not not-Spanish, and not not-Turkish and not not-Tatar. As I said, Zip is one of the greatest riddles in the world. He also has an amusing and gentle nature. And if any of you ladies and gentlemen wish to have the innocent pleasure of spitting in a stranger's face, you may do so. Zip is a simple man, a poor man. He won't be offended. But if any of you distinguished ladies and gentlemen wish to spit, you are requested to spit directly in Zip's face to avoid soiling his clothing. Our circus has spent a fortune to get clothes for Zip, the one and only complete and total idiot in the whole world. The Human Riddle. "Zip. *Who is he?*"

THE CROWD *(With a wild racket):* Hooray! Hooray for Zip!
(They start a spitting orgy.)
Zip: *(Smiles good naturedly and wipes himself off.)*

A LITTLE LADY: Can you spit on his nose?

ANOTHER: And in his eyes?

BARKER: Yes, you can, honourable ladies. But please, don't hit his clothes. They cost money. And now, we ask the audience to be going. It's getting late, and time to close the show.

CRIES FROM THE CROWD: Zip!

Freak!

Monkey!

(*The crowd chases after him to poke at him with sticks.* ZIP *stays calm, smiles. Only the Barker's speech saves him.*)

BARKER: Ladies and gentlemen. Please. Please. Stay calm. You can have as much innocent fun as you want. But we beg you, don't poke at him. He's our property. He costs money. (*Stands in front of him to protect him from the riled up masses.*)

CROWD: Freak! Zip! Monkey! Orangutan!

(*The lights go down and the crowd leaves.*)

(*The side-show folk gather around* ZIP. *They wipe him off with great respect. The Fat Lady kisses him. The Bearded Lady helps him out of his costume. They spray him with perfume. They dress him in a cape and top hat. They all make way for him. Meanwhile, The Bearded Lady takes the opportunity to kiss* FLOSSIE.)

ZIP *(Calm, very dignied):* Tell those two they can look for another job. This is no place for romance. Here, we work. *(To them.)* And when I pass by, all eyes should be on me. I have no use for insolent people. Oh, yes.

FLOSSIE AND BEARDED LADY *(They turn up their noses and snap their fingers in his face):* To hell with you I'll tell you what. We're going over to Menachem-Josef.

ZIP *(Hostile):* Go on then, by all means. Drop dead, *sonuvabitches!*

BARKER *(Bows like a lackey, hands him his coat and hat):* Your automobile awaits you outside, sir.

ZIP: *(Exits very slowly.)*

Curtain

Act III

Act III

Scoundrel Johnnie's office. Lots of telephones. Maps on the wall, lots and lots of ingenious machines. Electric signal lights in all sorts of colours blinking on and off.

ZIP *(Near him* CHARLIE, THE BARKER*):* The main thing is—gadgets. It doesn't matter if they save time or not. A gadget is a beautiful thing in itself, even if it doesn't work. For example, Charlie, this gadget with the signal lights I invented to tell me who's calling on the phone. If they owe money, it lights up green. But if it's your own wife, yellow. A lover, blue, and so on . . . The lighting effects themselves work quite well. But it doesn't have anything to do with the phone. *(Telephone rings. Green light comes on.)* Hello? Who? Huh? Genevieve? Madeleine? How are you? *Comment vous portez-vous? (Pauses conversation. To* CHARLIE.*)* See how reliable it is? They don't owe anything. It's a French dictionary. Heh heh. You know, one of those dictionaries you can take to bed with you. She's taught me a lot of French pretty quick. *(To her.)* Yes. *Je vous remercie*, darling. Tomorrow night at the Hotel Wyndham? Alright. Bring your bag. *Ooh-la-la! Je suis bien fâché.* But you know, in New York they won't let a man and a woman check in for the night without luggage. New York isn't Paris. Ha ha. Eh?

What? Ok. Goodbye. *(Tips his hat in a gentlemanly way.* CHARLIE, *too. They forget the lady is on the telephone)* Oh yes! I'm very busy. A lot of business, you know. *Au revoir! (Hangs up, speaks to* CHARLIE.*)* You see, Charlie, this Menachem-Josef of ours thinks he's a big deal. He forgets there's a Mister Zipkin in this world. Well, I'm not going to let him deal any longer, *no sir. Oh no.* It's true, he's got a good head, this Menachem-Josef, I'll give him that, but he doesn't scare me. We don't scare.

CHARLIE: We don't scare. Ever.

ZIP *(To* CHARLIE*):* Are there a lot of people in the waiting room?

CHARLIE: Three. Two men and a woman. The men came first. Shall I show them in?

ZIP: Let them in. Let's get ready. Have you heard any news about Menachem's Messiah? *(Picks his nose.)*

CHARLIE: That guy? They say he's pulling in barrels of gold.

ZIP: Really? Gold? Barrels? Pulling it in? Listen, now, listen. Let me think a minute. *(Puts his hand on his forehead.)* Don't call them in, Charlie. *(Thinks.)* Let me think this through a bit. *(Pause.)* You know what, Charlie?

Charlie: What?

Zip: We'll get our own Messiah—and a better one than Menachem's. Charlie, brother, we're going to deliver a modern Messiah. A Kovner Zionist with a monocle.

He'll speak English. A Messiah that can ride a motorcycle. A Messiah that can dance, a modern Messiah, in every sense of the word, as they say. I hear that our little Menachem's got a Messiah for men, so I'll get a Messiah for women.

CHARLIE: You think that'll work, a Messiah for women?

ZIP: You know the rule, Charlie, it's always better to sell to women than to men. Take a simple thing like doctors, for example. Who does better business? The ones who specialize in men's problems or the ones that specialise in women's problems? *(Enthusiastically.)* Charlie, my man, you know what this means? A Messiah for women? It means a double Messiah—one for both men and women. Because a Messiah that's going to be a hit with women—a young athletic good-looking Messiah— he'll be a hit with the men too, because every woman will, so to speak, be a promoter for our Messiah . . . . And this Messiah of ours, he doesn't come riding a horse or an ass. Like I've already told you, he comes riding a motorcycle—at seventy miles an hour. Oh yes! Not like that ruptured Jew, but a young he-man—a Douglas Fairbanks.[28]

CHARLIE: Do you already have someone or are you going to get someone?

ZIP: I've already got one.

CHARLIE: Already?

ZIP: Yes, I've got one.

CHARLIE: Just like that?

ZIP: Just like that.

CHARLIE: Where'd you dig him up? Who is he? What's his name?

ZIP: Dr. Shimen Kestleberg who's just arrived in America a week ago from Kovno. He's a Kovner. He actually came over to give speeches on behalf of the Zionist organization in America, but I don't think he'll object to having a little extra work on the side.

CHARLIE: What are you talking about? That guy's an idealist, a martyr.

ZIP: Well, yes. Since he's an idealist and a martyr, I'll have to pay him 150 dollars a week. If he weren't an idealist and a martyr, I could get him cheap. Heh heh heh. Since he's an idealist and a martyr, I'll have to throw in an extra hundred dollars a week. But it's worth it. Charlie, I think that a Zionist, a martyr understands business better than a regular Jew. Besides, our Messiah already has a lot of friends in the press—that's worth something too, no? (*Differently*) Call the people in. *Goodbye!*

CHARLIE: Goodbye.

(*The* INVENTOR *enters. He speaks quickly, asking questions and answering them himself.*)

INVENTOR: Well. Of course you'll permit me. Why wouldn't you permit? So I'll sit. Why not? Why wouldn't I sit?

That is, just so, eh? A train goes, yes? Of course it goes. Why wouldn't it go? And why does it go? Because it has steam. If it didn't have steam, it wouldn't go—true or not? True. And so it's like this. If you've got steam, you go. If you don't have steam, you don't go. Am I right or not? If so, then here's the question. Or not? So why doesn't a samovar go? The truth of it is just this—and that's what we're after—Samovars *should* go. And if you want to ride off, you should be able to sit yourself down on a samovar, and away you go. Do you get it? Of course you get it. And what do we gain from it? We gain eight things. First, you don't have to buy train tickets. Second: They won't have to print tickets. Third, you won't have to look for hot water to make tea. Because when a samovar goes, it heats up and when it whistles, it boils and when it boils, you throw in some tea-leaves and you can drink. On the one hand, you drink and on the other, you drive. That is to say, it drives, it drinks. You drink, you drive. How many's that so far?

CHARLIE: Three.

INVENTOR: Yes, that's three so far. Fourthly—but why talk? The less talk, the better. True or not? True. Here are the diagrams. *(Shows him the blueprints.)* Why did I come to you Mr. Zipkin and not to someone else? The truth of it is, as everyone knows, Mr. Zipkin likes patents, efficiency, inventions. It's no small thing, all of America will follow your lead. So should God help us. You'll soon be as popular as President Lincoln or Captain Dreyfus or Mary Pickford.[29] So. What do you say? Do you like it?

ZIP: That is a serious question, my dear Jew. This deserves

deep thought. *(Thinks.)* I'll tell you what. Leave your diagrams with us. Leave all your material. We'll think it over. Goodbye. I think it will be alright.

INVENTOR *(On the way out)*: *Adieu.* And let's hope that all America will soon be riding samovars. Or not? Why not? People will ride. And the more they ride, the more gold I'll be sitting on. Long live America! Hooray for America!

ZIP: Hooray.

CHARLIE *(Comes flying)*: Hip Hip Hooray!

(Music—a little bit like Yankee Doodle.)

NEW MESSIAH: *(Accompanied by two* REPORTERS.*)*

FIRST REPORTER: *(To the tune of Yankee Doodle.)*
Now, we're bringing you a Big Shot, Bringing joy to one and all. Soon—hooray—we will be dancing All around the Golden Bull.

ALL: Oh happy bull! Oh happy day.
Whoopee! Happy! Yippie!
Long live every Zionist!
Now that's good for business!

MESSIAH *(To* CHARLIE*)*: And with whom do I have the honour? *S'il vous plait. Reden Sie? . . . Sprechen Sie? . . . Beloshn ivris? . . . Yesh li—*[30]

CHARLIE: I'm just Charlie. That guy's the boss.

MESSIAH: The Gentlemen of the Press, if you please, have told me you're looking for a Messiah. Is that true?

ZIP: It's true.

MESSIAH: True? Yes? *(Motions to the* REPORTERS.*)* These are my agents. Five percent commission if the deal goes through, *bitte sehr, s'il vous plait. proszę panę. Bevakoshosa*

ZIP: Sit, gentlemen.

BOTH REPORTERS: We're sitting already. Just so we sit. We're already seated.

FIRST REPORTER: My name is Ab—ra—ham.

BOTH REPORTERS: Abe, Abe, Ham—Ham—Ham. Abra-ham.

SECOND REPORTER: And I'm called Moyshe.
Moy, Moy, Moy,
Sheh—Sheh—Sheh.
Moyshe.

MESSIAH: I think that all the same, for my part, I require no introductions. I am Dr.—*(Tries to shows his calling card.)*

ZIP: I know. I know.

MESSIAH: I am a great idealist.

ZIP *(With a sigh):* We know that, too.

CHARLIE *(Also with a sigh):* We know.

BOTH REPORTERS:
   He is a great idealist
   But makes a buck—he can't resist.

MESSIAH: I am, good sir, a martyr, just like Captain Dreyfus.

BOTH REPORTERS:
   Drey, Drey, Drey,
   Fus—Fus—Fus.
   Just like Dreyfus.

MESSIAH: Also like Mendel Beilis. *Wissen Sie?*

BOTH REPORTERS:
   Bei, Bei, Bei,
   Li. Li. Li.
   Es. Es. Es.
   Mendel Beilis.

MESSIAH *(To them):* So, *widzi pan.* I have a wife and two
   children and the children, *wissen Sie,* need to eat well
   and drink well and sleep well and have good minders.
   My wife likes to wear the best Parisian clothes, travel
   to the hot springs, play preferans, roulette, pinochle.
   (Pause.) My daughter, *proszę panę* needs a good horse
   to go riding in the Bois-de-Boulogne, *wissen Sie*! So be
   it. *Nichts zu machen.* It can't be helped.

BOTH REPORTERS:
Can't, Can't, Can't,
Be. Be. Be.
Can't be helped.

MESSIAH *(To them):* What's more, *widzi pan*, I've got a girl suing me for thirty thousand dollars damages. I supposedly stole her honour. So she says. *(Sarcastically.)* Her honour!

BOTH REPORTERS:
Aw, Aw, Aw,
Ner—Ner—Ner.
Stole her honour.

ZIP: So, in short?

CHARLIE: Altogether?

MESSIAH: It's very simple, *widzi pan*. I want 260 a week for redemption, good sir. Don't forget that I'm an idealist. Martyrs and idealists are in short supply in America. *Widzi pan*, America is the land of materialism.

BOTH REPORTERS:
Ma, Ma, Ma,
Ter—Ter—Ter.
Materialism.

(From here on, it goes quicker, melodramatic or sung.)

ZIP: I'll give you 110. *(He stands up and quickly sits back down.)*

MESSIAH *(Likewise):* I won't take 110.

REPORTERS *(Also likewise):*
> He won't take 110.
> 110 he won't take.

ZIP: I'll give 115.

MESSIAH: I won't take 115.

REPORTERS:
> He won't take 115.
> 115 he just won't take.

ZIP: I'll give 125.

MESSIAH: No.

ZIP: 150. And not one cent more.

MESSIAH: *Wie Sie wollen*! That's your business. *N'est-ce pas*? I will not redeem the People of Israel from exile for less than 200 dollars a week. Don't forget what an ancient people they are. And what a stubborn one. It's no joke, redeeming a people like that. And besides, there's expenses—gas for my motorcycle. Surely you don't expect a modern Messiah to come riding on an ass. *(In German.) Das wäre ja scheußlich*, and what if the donkey did something? Well! What a mess! *N'est-ce pas*? Of course!

REPORTERS: Here's our compromise offer. 175 dollars a week plus gasoline.

ZIP: Fine. It's a deal. But you supply the motorcycle. Bring your motorcycle here. Let's see if it works.

MESSIAH: Oh, that's rich! My own motorcycle? What am I, a Rockefeller? I have my own oil well? I want two hundred dollars a week and a motorcycle.

ZIP: A stubborn guy. *(Whispers with* CHARLIE.*)* Well, *alright.* It's a deal. What can you do? I'll give you my own motorcycle. It's a little bit used, but perfectly good.

MESSIAH *(Hesitates):* There's still the question of whether your motorcycle is in good working order.

ZIP: What? You don't believe me? You don't believe Zipkin? That's lovely. *(To* CHARLIE.*)* Get the motorcycle. Let him see for himself. *(Near the doorstep. Tries the bike. It works. Makes a clamour)*

CHARLIE: If we're agreed, then let's drink a toast. *(Brings liquor. They drink.)*

ZIP: *L'Chaim*! With God's help, good business.

MESSIAH *(Sung):* Mead is mead and schnapps is schnapps.

REPORTERS: So kick up your heels and give a hop.

MESSIAH: Give a kick with your feet, spin your head this-a-way

ALL: And let's all shout: Hip Hip Hooray!

MESSIAH: Alright then I'll try out the motorcycle myself.
Watch out. Out of the way. *(Exits.)*

REPORTERS:
Ever onwards with the news
Telling tales about the Jews.
Helter-skelter we scurry about
Trying to get a newspaper out.
Hooray. Hooray. Hooray.

ALL: In the paper today.

REPORTERS: For we're just cronies

ALL: At the bridegroom's party.

ZIP: Now we've got it! We'll show him, our little Menachem,
how to bring a Messiah. Call that a Messiah? We'll show
him a Messiah. And a modern Messiah, no less. And for
women, no less. And on a motorcycle, no less, at seventy miles an hour.

*(We hear noise from the motorcycle. Everyone rushes to the
door.)*

FIRST REPORTER: What is it?

SECOND: Flossie just slugged our *Daytsher*, Dr. Kestleberg,
our Kovner Messiah.

FIRST: What for?

SECOND: She says he seduced her.

ZIP: So. *He's* her seducer. The swine *(Starts for the door, then stops.)* Aahh, there's no point making a fuss about it. Business is business.

Curtain

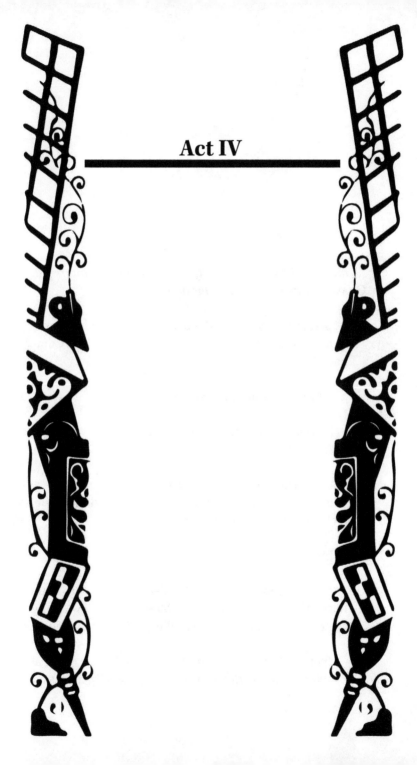

Act IV

Act IV

At the side show. It's still early, there are no spectators yet. CHARLIE *is helping* ZIP *into his outfit.*

ZIP: Can it really be? Has Menachem's gang really made a quarter of a million with their Messiah Holdings Company?

CHARLIE: That's what they say, Mr. Zipkin.

ZIP: Hmmm . . . With this Galitsianer character? With that *Yid*?

CHARLIE: I hear they're getting ready to go on a nation-wide tour with their Galitsianer Messiah and that little Jackie Bluffer'll be traveling with him.

ZIP: This is more serious than I thought.

CHARLIE: And that's not all. Little Menachem and his gang have taken out a patent on his Messiah. And if we bring our own, they'll hit us for a million dollars in damages.

ZIP *(Thinks):* That's a real problem, Charlie, a very real problem. *(Differently)* No, it's nothing. Legally, he has no grounds. He can't stop us. Menachem's outfit only has a patent on a Messiah with a beard. But our Messiah doesn't have a beard.

CHARLIE: Theirs doesn't have much of a beard left either. You'd be surprised how quick that simpleton degreened. Suddenly, their Galitsianer Messiah thinks he's the Sage of the Age.

ZIP: Well . . . He's a capable guy, this Galitsianer! You can't deny it: those Galitsianers are capable people. You've got to give him that. But I think our Kovno Messiah is better and we can beat their guy. First, because our Messiah is better looking. Second, he has better connections in the press. Third, he's a Zionist.

CHARLIE: They say the other guy's become a Zionist, too— maybe a Labour Zionist, don't remember.

ZIP: What are you saying? That's no good.

CHARLIE: My advice is, we should amalgamate. Have what they call a *moirger*. I hold with the rule that in unity, there is strength.[31] You've both got a gold mine. You don't have to divide your forces.

ZIP *(Pensively):* Ha? What did you say? Divide forces? That's true. Our forces *are* divided. Together, we could remake the world. Two Messiahs at the same time. One for women, one for men; one for intellectuals, one for the masses; one for the Americanised, one for immigrants. Do you understand what this means, Charlie? It means we can corner the market in Messiahs and shut out the possibility of any competition. It means not just money, but power and prestige. We redeem whoever we like, and if we don't like you, you don't get redeemed.

CHARLIE: From what?

ZIP: What's the difference, from what? We redeem them, and that's that. A redeemed man is a brand new man, Charlie. You know that yourself.

CHARLIE: An unredeemed man can't compare to a redeemed man, that's true. The thing is just . . .

ZIP: What?

CHARLIE: The thing is, if we come to him, to Menachem, and not him to us, he'll grab us by the throat and strangle us. You don't know our little Menachem. A cutthroat, a bandit.

ZIP: True enough, Charlie. But that's the whole point. It's *because* he's a bandit, a cut-throat, that we need him as a partner. He's talented, there's no denying it.

CHARLIE: Who's denying it? Menachem's a genius.

ZIP: Hmm . . . If he's a genius, what am I? A potted palm?

CHARLIE: You're a genius, too, but a different kind. Subtler. That guy's all flame and fire. He's a pickpocket.

ZIP: Bah, he's not such a threat. That guy just did it first and grabbed the patent. That's what the problem is. Oh, yes. That's not good, not good at all.

CHARLIE: If the court holds that his patent applies to all Messiahs, even those without beards, then—God forbid—we're over a barrel.

ZIP: We're not quite there yet. Luckily, I have some influence in court. I'm not saying it wouldn't be better to join forces. But we've got to make sure he doesn't get wind that we're behind him.

CHARLIE: Do you know what I think, Mr. Zipkin?

ZIP: What?

CHARLIE: This Messiah of theirs. I think we can undermine him a bit.

ZIP: I don't understand.

CHARLIE: It's simple. Since he's always proclaiming that his Messiah has come to redeem all classes—even Christians, we can take this to mean he's an internationalist. If so, how do we know he's not a Communist? And that he wasn't sent from Moscow by Comintern?[32]

ZIP: But there's the problem that he's a Galitsianer.

CHARLIE: That doesn't mean anything. He can be a Galitsianer working for the Comintern. Look at Karl Radek.[33]

ZIP: What are you saying? Karl Radek? The Bolshevik? Comintern?

CHARLIE: Of course, of course. And if he's a Bolshevik, he should be deported. Eh? What do you say to that, Mr. Zipkin?

ZIP: I'm not sure . . . Let's see . . . We'll keep that as a last resort. You forget, Charlie, that we'll have to get to the *Goyim*, too. You can't make a living from Jews alone. And you're forgetting another thing, Charlie—our Messiah is a Kovner and Kovno once belonged to Russia.

(Enter JACKIE BLUFFER*)*

JACKIE: Hello, Mr. Zipkin. Hello, Charlie.

ZIP: Hello.

CHARLIE: Hello. What's new?

JACKIE: Nothing. I was passing by and I thought, it's still early. There won't be any business yet. I'll stop by and see how things are going with you guys.

ZIP: With us, thank God, things are *alright*. How're things with you?

JACKIE: Also *alright*.

CHARLIE: *Alright?*

JACKIE: *Alright.*

(Pause.)

ZIP: And nothing new with you either?

JACKIE: With us? No. And with you?

CHARLIE: Nothing new with us, either. How's your Messiah doing?

JACKIE: How's he doing? It seems he's learned to play poker.

ZIP: And that's all the news?

JACKIE: You probably know we have a patent on him.

ZIP: How would I know that?

JACKIE: I thought you knew. Our patent is on all Messiahs for all time in all lands.

ZIP: Now if remember correctly, there's a rule in patent law that you can only patent the original. But if someone else comes along and improves on the article, the first guy's rights are null and void.

JACKIE: But, you have to show, precisely, without doubt, that the new article is an improvement on the old one. A step further, so to speak.

ZIP: We can do that.

JACKIE: You're a pretty smart guy, Mr. Zipkin. How can you say such a foolish thing? Who can prove that he has a better Messiah than us? And if he is better, what's better about him?

CHARLIE: What's better about him? He's better because—

ZIP: He's better because he's not a . . . *foreigner*, a greenie.

JACKIE: But is he a Jew? Then what's the difference?

ZIP: A great deal of difference. A Messiah who's been to college and can play football and dance the Black Bottom. Compared to a greenie Messiah who's carrying God knows what to infect America.

CHARLIE: My thoughts exactly.

JACKIE: What's he going to infect with? He doesn't have trachoma. He doesn't have tuberculosis either. And he doesn't have smallpox, either. And he's already had the measles, otherwise they wouldn't have let him into the country.

ZIP: That's not what I mean.

CHARLIE: That's not what we mean.

JACKIE: So what kind of infection could it be?

ZIP: I dunno . . . He could for example infect America with Bolshevism. I'm not saying it's true, God help us. But still, it could happen. Is he an internationalist? Does he redeem all walks of life and all nations? You, yourself, say as much. So what does that mean? It means his ideology is completely Bolshevistic. That is, I'm not saying it is, but it could be. That's what people are saying.

JACKIE: Am I crazy or are you crazy? What do you take me for? Crazy? What is this "Bolshevik"? That guy knows as much about Bolshevism as a chicken knows about Yom Kippur.[34]

ZIP: That doesn't mean anything. A person can be a Bolshevik and not even know it. And you know how much they like reds down in Washington. Especially greenie reds. You're probably familiar with the law regarding immigrants who are enemies of the state?

CHARLIE: What? You think Jack doesn't know? What do you think? He just arrived in America yesterday?

JACKIE: *(Pause)* Hear me out gentlemen. These things don't concern us here. I came to talk business, that is, I'm speaking not for myself, but for the firm of Menachem-Josef, which I represent.

ZIP: What kind of business could I have with Menachem-Josef? That guy's a fly-by-night. I'm different. I'm solid. A rock. A block of flint is what I am! Oh yes. I run a respectable business. With a solid foundation. A deep foundation. That's what kind of man I am. Menachem-Josef has made a lot of empty noise with his half-baked Messiah.

JACKIE: Half-baked?

ZIP: Half-a-Messiah. Half-a-Messiah. Maybe he'd be the real deal in Warsaw or Lemberg or Koidanov.[35] But not in New York. Not in America. Not in the Twentieth Century. Not in the Century of Progress. *(Pause.)* I have a Messiah.

CHARLIE: We have a Messiah.

ZIP: A young guy, with muscles. A heartthrob. A Zionist. With stature. An athlete. He's won prizes at football and weight-lifting. He's a second Samson. Yes. Yes. And furthermore ...

CHARLIE: And furthermore—

ZIP: Our Messiah won't come creeping on an ass like yours. He'll blast into New York on a motorcycle, accompanied by a squadron of firemen in yellow automobiles. Overhead, we'll be flying our airplane with a message written in smoke "Messiah Has Come. *He Is Here. The Newest Messiah. Latest Style. Up-To-Date Fashion. Comme il faut. Nothing Better.*"

JACKIE: Hmm... All very well said. If you have someone to bring on a motorcycle that is. If you have a Messiah so to speak.

ZIP: We already have one—

CHARLIE: We already have one—

JACKIE: I know you have a Messiah. The question is whether someone's going to put him in the slammer before he has a chance to come riding on a motorcycle.

ZIP: Who's going to put him in the slammer?

JACKIE: Well I'm not going to do it. He didn't defile *me*. He didn't rob *me* of my honour.

ZIP *(Startled):* And who did he defile?

JACKIE: A woman, apparently.

ZIP *(Feigns ignorance):* And who's the woman? If we might ask?

JACKIE: You might. It's no secret. In a couple of days everybody will know. The case is ready to go to court.

ZIP: So let's hear. Who's he supposed to have violated, this Kovno Messiah of ours?

CHARLIE: Who?

JACKIE *(Cool):* He violated the innocent Flossie who used to work in our office. *(Melodramatically)* He robbed her of her honour.

CHARLIE: Ha-ha! From *her* you have to rob it? My God. My God.

JACKIE: Please, please, please. Flossie is just as innocent as anyone else. Besides, she has a witness that she screamed. A clear-cut case of rape. You understand, that's apart from damages. Eighty thousand dollars for breaking her heart.

ZIP and CHARLIE *(Exchange glances):* Hmm . . . So that's how it is

Jackie: That's how it is.

(Pause.)

ZIP: You know what I'll tell you, Jack, nevermind this "de-file-shmefile" stuff. We're men. We know what this is about. And if it comes to court, I'll have something to say, too. And as to Flossie, Charlie has something to tell, too . . . Charlie?

CHARLIE: I know *I've* never slept with her, not even once.

ZIP: Shhh . . . No one's asking you.

CHARLIE: And you think I'm worried about people saying our Messiah's a Communist. Ridiculous.

JACKIE: Perhaps. But the bad press alone can put a shadow on business. Even if it comes out later that there was nothing to it. So I ask you, do we have good merchandise? There's only two of us at the fair. Both capable men. Both businessmen.

CHARLIE: Geniuses!

JACKIE: Geniuses!

ZIP: Both honourable men! Both men who understand business. So why the hell do we need to be in competition? I have a Messiah for women—you have a Messiah for men—Good! I have an Americanised Messiah, you have a greenie—Fine! You're a theatre producer, I have a side-show— Fine! Say . . . You know what just occurred to me? It's just occurred to me we could have a prize fight, a boxing-match between the two Messiahs. Right here at the side-show. A boxing match between two Messiahs. First, for the publicity. Second, we can make a buck. What sport wouldn't pay fifteen dollars for a ticket to see two Messiahs fight it out? That's number one. Then we get another pay-off right after the fight we'll write the loser off as a False Messiah, and we'll be left with the True Messiah—the winner. We make out on two fronts. One, we establish our Messiah Cartel on solid ground. One man instead of two; two, we don't have to pay the other guy. We save half the cost. And three, we shut out any further competition. They'll be scared to fight us.

JACKIE: All in all, I like it. I'll run straight to Mr. Menachem-Josef with this and we'll see what we can do. This whole business with the fight—it's got me hooked. It's a great idea—A fight between two Messiahs! No small thing! One Messiah slugs. The other, a solid blow. Right in the snout. Bam! One with a bloody nose. The other with a black eye. Haha. If that don't put America back on its feet, I don't know what will.

CHARLIE: It'll do it, it'll do it. It'll rock the nation. We'll pile up mountains of cash. Not to mention the glory! The glory! No small thing, glory.

ZIP *(Delighted):* A fight between two Messiahs! Even America has never seen the likes of that.

JACKIE: So, gotta run. Goodbye. Goodbye.

ZIP: So, we can open. Make some noise out there. *(Yells.)* Look alive! *(Noise. People start to pour in. More noise. Curtain falls for several seconds.)*

CHARLIE: *Ladies and gentlemen* don't go away. Don't go away. The show is about to begin. *(Automatically.) Big Show. Big Show. Biggest Show in Coney Island. (Helps Flossie down from the broom. She disappears off the rope inside.)*

CHARLIE *(Quietly to* FLOSSIE*):* Send in your boyfriend, the Bearded Lady. And take the broom.

(Enter JIM*)*

JIM *(A tall, thin boy with a beard. Smokes a long-stemmed pipe):* Well?

SCOUNDREL JOHNNIE: Dammit, put out the pipe. Your mouth is going to stink, Jim. You forget that you're a woman. *(Tragic.)* Man, if somebody decides to cop a feel, I'm in big trouble. Have you put on your *jock-strap* at least? Women come up and talk to you. You've got to be careful. Heaven forbid, I should be so unlucky. You can't let the audience, God forbid, find out you're a fake. We'll be kaput. *(Yells.)* Our luck could run out. They're watching us with a thousand jealous eyes. Just waiting for us to fail.

JIM: Why are you yelling, Mr. Zipkin? You can speak quietly.

ZIP: I'll yell. If you had sixty-thousand dollars invested in this business, you'd yell, too. And you show up without a girdle.

JIM: Who told you I'm not wearing a girdle? Go ahead, feel. (ZIP *gives a feel. Calms down.*) Don't worry. I didn't forget. (*Grumbles.*) I'm getting sick of this whole circus thing. For this lousy business I've got to pay for a girdle. (*Gets dressed, plumps up his breasts.*) That's all I need. I need this like I need a burst appendix. Why did I give up being a photographer? Did I earn so badly? And it was fun. (*Remembers.*) I scared that Messiah to death. (*Imitates.*) "Yankel, tell him not to hurt me." "Do I have to, Yankel?" "Well, you gotta do what you gotta do." (*Differently*) I'd like to see him now, that greenie zealot, Menachem-Josef's Messiah. A real big shot these days. He's filthy with money now. (*Sad.*) And me? Moron. that I am, I went and became the Bearded Lady. That guy at least has made a name for himself with his beard. A well-known Jew. And me? A fraud. A Coney Island fake. Like the *goy* who's half man, half woman. Poor thing. They cut off one of her breasts. A victim of cancer. So she shows the flat breast, it's supposed to be the male side, and the other side, the woman's. Devil take it. A deathly sick woman and she has to make a living showing her troubles. (*Shudders.*) Brrrr . . . . You and your Coney Island.

ZIP: *My* Coney Island? Why on earth mine? All America is Coney Island, fool. Fake, swindle, *bluff*—that's what America is built on. From the earliest times, people have wanted bread and circus. Today they want the same. And the less bread, the more circus you've got to give them. So we give it to them, we give them circus. Circus is so much cheaper than bread. Especially a Coney Island circus. *(Rubs his hands.)* I'm not complaining, brother.

JIM: Well, yes . . . If you work as a freak, I understand. You make a good living from it, live in luxury, have your own villa by the sea, drive a Packard automobile. But me? What do I get out of it? Thirty dollars a week. It's all Flossie's fault. She says, it's not nice to be an ordinary worker, a photographer. Find a better job, more genteel, she says. Now I've got to fuss around with this stuff. *(Pokes his breasts.)*

ZIP *(Helps him with his outfit):* Don't grumble, brother. Don't grumble. You have a good job and you earn an honest penny. *(Yells.)* Noise! Make some noise! What are you? Asleep there?

JIM: The Ossified Man makes more than me. And he doesn't work at all. He just lies there, dying peacefully, waiting for his heart to turn to stone. That's work? But somehow, he makes fifty dollars more than me. And even the woman with her breast cut off makes more than me. What? She has cancer, so just because I don't have cancer, I can't make a living?

ZIP: You forget, brother, that he and the Fat Lady are the

only ones in our circus who aren't fakes. Besides. You think I want to pay the Ossified Man so much? But what can you do? He's the only one at the fair. How many people do you know whose blood is turning to stone? I'll tell you the truth. I'm worried about what I'm going to do six months from now when he dies. He's our main attraction. Aside from me, aside from Zip. Without me, the circus isn't worth a plugged nickel. Everyone'll tell you that, Jim. And you know it too, Jim. Oh yes. All Coney Island knows it. That the circus depends on "Zip", The Human Riddle, the "What is it?",[36] as I called myself. "Zip? What is it?" That name makes money.

JIM: I'm a bigger attraction than the woman with cancer. There aren't a lot of Bearded Ladies. Especially not with beards as long as mine. *(Strokes his beard.)*

ZIP: Here's what I say: take care of your beard. Look after it and it'll earn you respect. Don't forget, your strength lies in your beard.

JIM: You think I don't take care of it? At night, I keep it in a pouch. In the morning, I wash it. By day, I sun it, so it'll turn blond. What else can I do?

ZIP: I'm not criticising you. I'm just saying that if a man wants to work his way up, he can't be lazy. We live in a great country, Jim, a great land. A real talent won't go to waste. Take the champion spitter from Philadelphia for example. He makes over a million dollars a year. Or take me, Jim. What was I eight years ago? A poor kid, a street urchin, with my belly button on display. Until I had the brilliant idea to become a freak. From then on, I was *alright.* Oh yes. I thought like this: inside every man, there's a little bit of a freak. But he's ashamed to show it. So if they see a real freak, they whinny like horses, they squeal with delight like a child that sees itself in the mirror for the first time. "Brother, be a freak," I told myself. "You'll be a man and eat in style." I thought, if a crooked guy like Menachem-Josef can make a million dollars, you should be able to make more. A lot more. You'll out-do him. Oh yes. You, Mr. Zipkin, you will bury him so good, they'll never find him. You'll *beat him to pieces* as we say in America.

JIM *(Jealous):* Well. Who could compare with you, Mr. Zipkin? You're a genius. We should all be so lucky. That's not a compliment. But the truth is . . .

ZIPKIN *(Barely hears what Jim is saying):* Oh, people will laugh. Let them laugh. Silently, I'm laughing at them. They give me their pennies and they're bigger freaks than we are, Jim. It's just that they don't get paid for it, and we do. *(Yells outside.)* Noise. Noise. Noise! What are you? Asleep out there for God's sake? *(Almost automaticly.)* Big Show, Big Show, Biggest Show in Coney Island.

(Pause.)

ZIP *(Delves further into his apologia):* Yes. So what if they spit in my face? They spit in my face. I hold that this whole life is being spit in the face and cast aside. I'm telling you, Jim. Me. "Zip". The Greatest Freak on Earth. Me. The Human Riddle, the "What Is It?", boss of this here whole side-show. Me, who's worth over a hundred thousand dollars. I'm telling you. Oh yes. This whole life is one big spit in the face. Beyond that, what difference does it make whether it's our own spit inside our cheeks or someone else's outside our cheeks. It's all the same, Jim. All the same. Abraham Lincoln said, "You can fool some of the people all of the time, and all of the people some of the time, but you can't fool all of the people all of the time." I say the opposite. Like the great circus man P.T. Barnum, I say, "You can fool all of the people all of the time." Oh yes. People are children: the more you fool them, the more they love you. I believe in *bluff*. The God of Bluff is the greatest God on earth, Jim! Greater than Jesus of Nazareth, greater even than Edison or Ford. He is the only God and you should pray to him with all your heart. Otherwise you're nothing. Otherwise you won't be a success. I made a pact with myself: I won't serve old Daddy Jehovah and not his baby boy Jesus, either. I will serve only Him—The Yellow One, the Almighty, who is pure tongue, pure ear, pure desire, pure appetite, pure life. Do you understand, Jim? They think I bluff for the sake of money. They're wrong. I'm an idealist: I bluff for the sake of bluff. For example, I established a joint-share company and sold shares in my circus with the aim of fleecing people. I was sure the company would go bankrupt in a few months. But it turned out the opposite. The business started to pay. And as president of the joint-share company, I should have declared a dividend. But it just didn't feel right. True, I said to myself, I could earn more if I don't declare bankruptcy . But it's not about the money—it's a matter of principle! And my principle was bluff; I really suffered when things didn't go as planned *(Poetically.)* Oh yes. I am not a man without principle, Jim. I want you to know that.

JIM: I know. I know, Mr. Zipkin. You don't need to tell me.

ZIPKIN *(With a deep sigh):* I've got to change for work. The *show* is about to begin. *(Outside, it's getting louder.)* Today is a hot Sunday and they . . . nothing . . . *(Gestures to the musicians outside.)* They're asleep. The papers say we'll get half a million people in Coney Island today. *(As if to himself. Licks his lips at the thought)* Oh, I love a day like this. *(Descriptively)* It's hot. Almost suffocating. You sweat. The crowd sweats. You swear. You can't stand each other. The beast is aroused—it must be entertained. Bread! Circus! Cheap side-show! Coney Island! *One dime, ten cents.* More than ten cents at a time, they won't give you, the poor devils! But ten-cent-pieces, they'll give you as many times as you can fool them. And the dimes become dollars, and the dollars become hundreds, and the hundreds become millions. And if you've got a million, you're *alright.* And with a couple of million, I, "Zip", can be President of America, President of the richest republic in the world. And they're asleep. *(Gestures outside.)* They don't care. They're asleep. *(Yells.)* Hey! What are you? Asleep out there? Can't you see? They're falling down in the street in this heat. *(Happy.)* What a day! What a day! Only nine o'clock and you can't breathe. *(Yells louder.)* Hey there, *boys,* look alive!

(A fearful noise from all sorts of instruments.)

Curtain

Act V

Act V

The same scene. The two Messiahs are preparing for the fight. Menachem's Messiah is saying prayers. Menachem, Flossie and Jack are gathered around him.

FLOSSIE: *(Chews gum.)*

JACKIE: Do you know the rules, uncle? No hitting below the belt.

MESSIAH: Is he wearing a belt?

MENACHEM: I mean, not below the penis.

MESSIAH: And can you hit the penis itself?

MENACHEM: Heaven forbid! What are you saying? It's against the law. American Law is on the side of . . . the . . . penis.

MESSIAH: Well, if you've gotta hit above the penis, you've gotta. *(Groans.)* Only God help me, I should have the strength.

JACK: Get ahold of yourself, uncle. Get angry. Don't for-

get—the other guy's trying to take away your livelihood.

MESSIAH: What a rotten life! Live-li-hood. *(Looks for
something under his shirt at his neck.)*

FLOSSIE: What are you looking for?

MESSIAH: It's an amulet that my mother—peace be
upon her—gave me so that she could watch over me
throughout my life. *(Pulls out an amulet.)*

FLOSSIE *(Quietly):* What good's an amulet? It's about as
much good as giving aspirin to a dead man. I have a
better amulet for you. Here. *(Takes a horseshoe from
under her shawl.)*

MESSIAH: What's this?

FLOSSIE: Shhhh . . . It's a horseshoe. Americans believe a
horseshoe is lucky. Ask Charlie Chaplin, he'll tell you.[37]

MESSIAH: Aha. I understand. That's why they have horse-
shoes over their doors. Aha. So that's it. I always won-
dered about that.

FLOSSIE: Yes. *(Pause.)* Take it, Mr. Messiah. A horseshoe is
a good luck charm for winning a fight.

MESSIAH: *(Takes the horseshoe, goes to put it in his pocket.)*

FLOSSIE: No, not in your pocket; put it here *(She puts it in
his glove.)*

MESSIAH: May it be so. I hope at least it's a good charm, dear God *(Groans.)* What a miserable live-li-hood!

FLOSSIE: It will bring good fortune, Mr. Messiah. Never fear.

(During this time, the other MESSIAH *has been preparing for the fight. The four reporters are standing around the platform where the fight will take place with their photographic equipment.* ZIP *and the referee are saying something to the* YOUNG MESSIAH. OLD MESSIAH *in* tales kotn[38] *kisses his prayer book. Puts it away. Prepares himself. Prays. The* YOUNG MESSIAH *performs gymnastic exercises.)*

JACKIE *(To the* OLD MESSIAH*):* Get angry, uncle.

OLD MESSIAH: Do I have to be angry, Jack? Why? What good will it do me?

JACK: Like you always say, you gotta do what you gotta do. Without anger, you'll never win. You won't have a chance.

OLD MESSIAH: So, it means I've gotta be angry? Well, what you've gotta do, you've gotta do. *(Sighs.)* What a rotten life! *(Differently.)* Why should I be angry with him? Has he done something to me, Jackie?

JACK: Of course he's done something. He's going after your bread, your livelihood, uncle.

OLD MESSIAH: What a miserable life. My livelihood. Such a . . . Such a . . . I'll show him.

JACK *(Slaps him on the back):* 'Attaboy! That's the way. Bravo!

ZIP *(to* YOUNG MESSIAH*):* You understand, the loser doesn't just lose money. He also loses his career as Messiah. Remember that. That little Jew trying to take away your bread; he's out to ruin you. And who is he? A greenie Jew, a bumpkin, an ignoramus, a little Galitsianer.

YOUNG MESSIAH *(Smiles):* It's *alright*, Mr. Zip! Don't upset yourself. Please. We'll tear him apart in the first round. You can rely on me. It's *alright*. We'll squash him like a ripe apple. God help me, It's a pity about his wife and kids. But whose fault is it? A ruptured Jew like that, trying to—

ZIP: Don't be so sure of yourself. You never know. I've seen these little Jews. To look at them, I wouldn't give a plugged nickel for them, but when push comes to shove, they have the strength of iron. Don't mess around with these little Galitsianer Jews. They're not men, they're bandits.

CHARLIE: You'd be better off being angry with him. Without anger you can't do anything. Do as I say.

ZIP: Hatred is a great strength in itself. Why do you think the Jewish race has outlived all its enemies and given them, so to speak, a historical *knockout*? Because they viewed them with hatred. Hatred is the greatest strength. Hatred and anger.

YOUNG MESSIAH *(Angrier at being lectured than against his opponent)*: Enough of that. Enough of that. Stop giving me advice. You're making me nervous. God-Damn-Je-sus-Christ-*Donnerwetter*-Two-Times-Over!

(The bell sounds onstage.)

JACKIE: Ladies and gentlemen! I don't have to tell you that today's prize- fight is, so to say, that is, historic. In America, we've already had fights between Jews and Negroes, between Irishmen and Germans, between Russians and Frenchmen, between Americans and Chinese. But a fight between Messiahs is completely new. As never seen before. A thing such as the American intelligentsia has never before witnessed. The fight will take place in nine rounds. Mr. Messiah number zero weighs in naked at 145 pounds. *(Indicates the* OLD MESSIAH.*)* Messiah number double zero *(Indicates the* YOUNG MESSIAH.*)* weighs precisely three pounds more. Both are middle-weights. The winning Messiah will come out of this one of the greatest figures in boxing history. His head will be crowned with the laurels of glory. *(Pause.)* Today's fight was arranged by the distinguished impresarios Mr. Zip-kin *(*ZIPKIN *bows.)* and Mr. Menachem-Josef *(Bows.)* Both are well-known showmen and businessmen. Only through the cooperation of two such geniuses *(Indicates* ZIP *and* MENACHEM-JOSEF. *The two hold hands and bow.)* and by combining the capital of two such famous financiers has it been possible to bring to the American intelligentsia an evening of such high-qual-ity entertainment. Today's prize-fight will open with a prayer by the Reverend Doctor Rabbi Stefan Schwartz of Temple Loy-Lonu-Eil![39]

RABBI: *(Mumbles a prayer)*

OLD MESSIAH: *Borkhu-borkhshmoy, omeyn.*

YOUNG MESSIAH: Amen.

(The fight begins.)

VOICES:
Let him have it!
Hit him in the eye!
Get him in the rib.
Tear his guts out.
Murder him.
Kill him.
Kill the old Messiah.
Kill the young Messiah.
Kill em.
Kill em.

(The old Messiah wins very quickly. A great hoorah. They raise him up in the air.)

OLD MESSIAH *(Realises what a dirty thing he's done):* Oh horrible! I beat him bloody. *(Can't look.)*

JACK: It's nothing, uncle, it's nothing. It's what you've gotta do; this is America.

FLOSSIE: *(Goes to the* OLD MESSIAH *to kiss him. He won't let her.)*

OLD MESSIAH: Do I have to kiss girls, Jackie?

JACK: You have to, uncle, you have to.

OLD MESSIAH: Well, you've gotta do what you've gotta do.
(*Lets her kiss him. It gives him a belly ache.*)

JACK: *Ladies and gentlemen,* let me present to you the man who deserves all the credit for today's spectacle. That is, not he alone, but also Mr. Zipkin. (ZIP *bows.*) Both deserve our greatest appreciation because they spared neither money nor effort to arrange the greatest *fight* of all times and of all lands. A fight which must bring honour to American citizens in general and especially to us Israelites whose history goes back to Jerusalem, to Zion, to the shores of Lebanon, to the Jordan River and to the Wailing Wall. And now, *ladies and gentlemen,* none other than Mr. Menachem-Josef himself will speak to you, in person. (*Signals with his hands for him to come up. Nothing happens. Makes a sign to the musicians they should play the American National Anthem and that everyone should stand*)

MENACHEM-JOSEF: *Ladies and gentleman.* Well, it made a racket. The fight between the two Messiahs. The True Messiah (*Gestures to the* OLD MESSIAH.) and the False Messiah (*Gestures to the* YOUNG MESSIAH, *who is lying on the floor bleeding from open wounds.*) has ended honourably. The laurels go to him, the victor who has poured glory on our nation as much as on his own head. (*Places the wreath on his head.*) Today's prize-fight has shown once again that even in a fight between men, physical strength does not play as great a role as wisdom. Our Messiah fought with wisdom. (MESSIAH *holds the glove with the horseshoe and rubs it.*) That's why he has emerged victorious. The other one (*gestures*) fought without wisdom, without understanding, and so, he has come to disgraceful defeat. But it serves him right. He should never have, he ought never to have permitted himself, to enter into combat with such a holy man, such a divine man, who redeems all, whether for cold hard cash or on credit, that is, on the instalment plan. (*Pause.*) Today's victory establishes our one-and-only Messiah on par with the greatest people in the land— like Jack Dempsey, Willard, Fitzsimmons,[40] Kid McCoy, President Coolidge, and I believe, that for the American nation, whether Jewish or Christian, there can be no greater honour than to be redeemed by a Messiah who is in addition to being a Messiah, a gentleman and a fighter, a Messiah who lives an upstanding family life and puts money in the bank so he won't be a burden to his children in his old age. I thank you. (*Remembers.*) Yes, the young Messiah is dead, Long live the new Messiah! Hooray! (*Pause.*) What else was I going to say? Yes, let us all stand and sing our National Anthem.

(*The audience stands. They sing Hatikvah[41] to the tune of Yankee Doodle.*)

Curtain

<u>Notes</u>

1   **Grey** is *Der Tog. Der Tog* styled itself as the newspaper for the Jewish intelligentsia. It was the first Yiddish newspaper to include female journalists on its staff. Many of the great poets and writers appeared in its pages, including David Pinski, Aron Glanz-Leyeles, H. Leivick, Joseph Opatoshu and Anna Margolin. Later, we hear that Grey is "a little like blue and a little like white", a swipe at its support for Zionism.

  Black is the Orthodox paper, *Morgn Zhurnal.*

  Yellow is Abe Cahan's *Forverts*, a much beloved target of the Left, here caricatured as yellow journalism. At its height, it was one of the largest newspapers in the country with a circulation of 200,000.

2   **Menachem-Mendl:** a reference to the Sholem Aleichem character, a stereotypical ineffectual wheeler and dealer.

3   **Treyf:** non-kosher.

4   **Jack Dempsey** (1895–1983) Famous American boxer, he is considered one of the all- time greats. He held the World Heavyweight Championship from 1919 to 1926. The fight

in which he lost this title was attended by over 120,000 people. Perhaps relevant in this context is that along with Irish and Cherokee, his ancestry was part Jewish.

Chaim Weizmann (1874–1952) Biochemist, Zionist leader, a founder of Hebrew University and the Chaim Weizmann Institute of Science. He became the first President of Israel, after Albert Einstein showed he actually was smart and turned down the job, all far in the future at the time of the play. The story goes that Weizmann met Balfour in 1906. Balfour wanted to know why Weizmann thought Uganda unacceptable as a Jewish homeland. "Would you give up London for Paris?" Of course the answer was no. "London is our capital!" "Jerusalem was our capital when London was still a marsh." Weizmann invented an industrial process using bacteria to create acetone. This was the second such bio-industrial process. The first was alcohol production. His process was critical to the British in World War I and this gave him access to the political elite.

Morris Schwartz (1889–1960) Was a famous actor and theatrical producer. His Yiddish Art Theater was considered the crème de la crème of Yiddish theater. In addition to Yiddish plays, he produced classic playwrights including Shakespeare in Yiddish translation. His credits as a film producer include the 1939 film *Tevye*.

Menahem Mendel Beilis (1874–1934) In 1911 Beilis, a Russian Jew was accused of the murder of a Russian Gentile boy, Andrei Yuschinsky. Yuschinsky's religion is very much to the point here. A police detective, Nikolai Krasovsky, was able to determine that Beilis was not the murderer and was able to determine who the murderers were. He was fired when he refused to participate in the false accusations against Beilis. When his findings were published he was prosecuted but acquitted at trial. Beilis spent two years in prison awaiting what was to be a famous trial of the era. Both the prosecution and defense teams were among the most celebrated lawyers of the Russian bar. The prosecution's case centered around the blood libel, the slander that Jews must slaughter a Christian to use their blood in the manufacture of matzoh. Their star witness was an antisemitic priest named Justinas Pranaitis who presented himself as a religious expert in Jewish ritual. Panaitis testified that Yuschinsky's murder was a ritual murder citing the thirteen stab wounds on the body. Among the witnesses for the defense were Orthodox Christian philosopher Alexander Glagolev of the Kiev Theological Seminary and the Rabbi of Moscow, Rabbi Mazev. Panaitis' testimony fell apart on cross examination. His credibility was further damaged when it turned out that there were, in fact, fourteen stab wounds on the body. Beilis was acquitted.

Fearing for their safety, the Beilis family emigrated to Palestine and after several years came to America. His funeral was covered by the New York Times and was attended by four thousand mourners.

Act I

5   **The Golden Peacock** is a traditional symbol of Jewish creativity. Here it suggests a folkish content-free theatrical extravaganza. However, Nadir is having a bit of fun here: it's the title of his friend Moyshe-Leyb Halpern's second volume of poetry. The reference goes one level deeper. Halpern's *Golden Peacock* contains a poem called *Leyzer Elia* referencing a satirical character of Moyshe Nadir's.

6   By comparison, a ticket to see *Messiah In America* cost 35 cents.

7   **Galitsia**: A region straddling Poland and Ukraine. The name goes back to the early thirteenth century when the region was briefly held by Hungary. The great geographic / cultural / linguistic divide among Ashkenazi Jews is between Galitsianers and Litvaks. In *On The Eve*, Bernard Wasserstein cites the stereotypes that the Litvak was smart, analytical, learned, worldly, skeptical, proud, stubborn, dynamic, energetic, dry, rational, and unemotional while by contrast, the Galitsyaner was warm hearted, sly, witty, sharp, stingy, crafty, and something of a trickster. "To be called a [. . .] Galitzianer was for long not much of a compliment [. . .] It denoted folksy backwardness and at times also a petty mercantile mentality and moral shiftiness." And if that weren't damning enough, Galitsianers even put sugar in their gefilte fish!

8   **Peyes**: Sidelocks worn by Orthodox Jewish men.

9   **Daytsh**: (lit: German) usually denotes a Jew who has adopted a modern secular lifestyle. *Daytshke* = a female *Daytsh*.

10 Like the United States, Argentina saw a wave of Jewish immigration starting in the 1880s. By 1920, the Jewish population of Argentina numbered 150,000, making this the largest Jewish population in South America.

11 **Lemberg**, aka, Lviv, Lvov. Lemberg had been the capital of Galicia and during the interwar period, it was the third largest city in Poland and a major cultural and intellectual center. From Reb Simcha's viewpoint, this is the big city.

12 **Keyneynhore**: (lit: no Evil Eye).

13 **Kid McCoy** (1872–1940) Kid McCoy was a flamboyant boxer, known for a corkscrew punch. In addition to his boxing career (eighty-one wins) he appeared on stage and

in films. His personal life was a disaster. He married ten times. He suffered from alcoholism. In 1924, a woman who was enamored of him and was divorcing her husband was found dead of a single gunshot wound to her head. The morning after her death he held up an antique store and its customers. He claimed his paramour committed suicide, but was convicted of her manslaughter. He had recently been paroled at the time of the play.

14   By comparison, 1932 average weekly wages in the men's clothing industry were $22.47 for a 44 hour work week.

15   This is a considerable exaggeration. In 1936, the Zloty was on the gold standard, equal to 0.1687 grams of gold. 500 Zlotys would have been worth over a hundred dollars.

16   **Moishe Montefiore** (1784–1885) Born in Italy to a London Jewish family. He rose to great wealth and influence as a stockbroker and devoted much of his life to philanthropy. Among his honors, he was appointed Sheriff of London and was knighted by Queen Victoria. Jackie Bluffer uses him to persuade his uncle to allow his picture to be taken. There are many portraits of Moses Montefiore including oil paintings and engravings, but I have not been able to find his photograph.

There is a story that he was once seated next to an antisemitic nobleman at a banquet who said, "I have just returned from Japan, where they have neither pigs, nor Jews." Montefiore replied, "Then we should both go so they will have a sample of each."

17   Presumably a reference to Hecker's Flour founded in 1843. The company survives to this day as Heckers and Ceresota, having joined with its younger brother Ceresota, founded in 1891.

18 **Po'alei Zion**, a proletarian Zionist movement founded in Russia in the late nineteenth century. It spread to the Austrian Empire, the United States, England, Argentina, Romania and Palestine. It split into left and right camps, with the left unsuccessfully trying to join the Third International and the right becoming part of Zionist Socialists. Its newspaper, *Der Yidisher Kemfer*, founded in the early twentieth century persisted into the twenty-first.

19 **Sabbetai Zevi**: A play by the controversial Yiddish author Sholem Asch (1880-1957) concerning the historical false messiah Sabbatai Zevi (1626–1676).

   Sabbatai Zevi first claimed to be the Messiah in 1648. A Jewish mystical tradition had predicted this year for the coming of the Messiah. He again proclaimed himself Messiah in 1651. This time a supporter produced a forged "ancient" document prophesying his Messiahship. In 1658 he married a prostitute, a young woman who had been orphaned as a child in the Chmielnicki massacres ten years previously. This was seen as confirmation of his messiahship. Indeed, his defiance of religious law—for example celebrating fast days as feasts—was taken as paradoxical proof of his piety.

   At the height of his career, he had over a million followers. This all came to a crisis when the Sultan offered him the choice between death and conversion to Islam. He chose the latter bringing shame and disillusion to the vast majority of his followers. However, some of his followers saw this as a further paradoxical proof that he was the true Messiah. This was seen as either a deeper degradation that the Messiah must take upon himself before the ultimate redemption, or a ruse to convert Muslims to Judaism. These things die hard. A community of believers—Sabbateans—persisted into the twentieth century.

ACT II

20 **Yortsayt**: (often spelled "Jahrzeit" in English) The anniversary of a person's death, often a parent.

21 **Landslayt**: plural of "landsman" a fellow Jew who comes from the same Eastern European district or town.

22 **Kovno**: (modern day Kaunas) was the inter-war capital of Lithuania.

23 **Kapusta**: Cabbage, sauerkraut.

24 **"Hit the Nigger"**: Also known as "Hit the Coon" or "African Dodger" was a real-life carnival game popular in America during the early decades of the twentieth century.
     When attempts were made to ban the game (due to frequent serious injuries) the "African Dip" was developed where hitting a target caused the victim to fall into a water tank.

25 **"kh'hob dikh in dr'erd"**: A standard Yiddish curse, approximately, "Go to hell!" or "Drop dead!"

26 **Evelyn Nesbit** was the stage name of Florence Evelyn Nesbit (1884–1967). The name here is chosen for its association with scandal. Evelyn Nesbit was a famous chorus girl,

artists' model and "Gibson Girl". She claimed to have been drugged and raped by the architect Stanford White. She was no more than sixteen and may have been as young as fourteen at the time so White would have been nearly three times her age. In spite of this, she kept up a relationship with White. She was later romantically involved with John Barrymore and later was pursued by Harry Kendall Thaw. On a European trip Thaw interrogated her about her treatment at the hands of Stanford White. On the same trip, he imprisoned her in an Austrian castle where he beat her and took advantage of her sexually. In spite of this, she ultimately married him.

A year later on a hot summer night, Thaw murdered White towards the close of a theatrical performance on the roof of Madison Square Garden. In the ensuing media frenzy, the press dubbed this 1906 murder "the crime of the century."

27 **The Daughters of the American Revolution**: Famously reactionary, classist and racist. At the time of Messiah, the DAR did not admit African Americans as members or allow them to perform at its halls. It was only three years after Messiah that the DAR refused to allow Marion Anderson to perform at Constitution Hall. In the ensuing kerfuffle, Eleanor Roosevelt resigned her membership the DAR and Anderson wound up performing in front of the Lincoln Memorial. It was not until 1977 that they admitted their first black member and as late as 1984 when a chapter refused membership to a qualified African American the national organization refused to overrule them.

ACT III

28 **Douglas Fairbanks**: Screen name of Douglas Ullman (1883–1939). He began his Hollywood career under D. W. Griffith.

He quickly became one of the most popular and most highly paid actors in Hollywood. In order to maintain artistic and financial control over their work, he, along with Mary Pickford, Charlie Chaplin and D. W. Griffith founded United Artists. He is famous for swashbuckling films full of derring-do.

29 **Alfred Dreyfus** (1859–1935) came from a French family of assimilated Jews. He was the protagonist of *l'affaire Dreyfus*. In 1894 he was a captain in the French Army when a secret military document was provided to the Germans. Dreyfus was accused of treason and sentenced to life imprisonment. The conviction relied on a secret trove of documents, most of which had been forged by Maj. H. J. Henry. By 1896, the new head of the intelligence service Lt. Col. Jacques Picart became aware that there was a miscarriage of justice and was able to determine that the actual culprit was Maj. Ferdinand Esterhazy. However, Henry forged additional documents which carried the day and Picart was dismissed from his post. In one of the most dramatic moments of the case, the world famous novelist Emile Zola published an open letter to the president of the republic accusing the anti-Dreyfusards of libel. This letter was famously titled J' accuse . . . ! and occupied the entire front page of the newspaper *L'Aurore*. Compounding the original travesty of justice, Zola was tried and convicted of libel. In 1898, when Henry's forgeries were discovered, he was arrested and committed suicide in his cell. At this point, Dreyfus' innocence should have been clear to all, but he was again put on trial and convicted. It would be 1906 before Dreyfus' innocence was fully legally established.

During this time *l'affaire Dreyfus* consumed French politics. It gave license to antisemitic forces throughout French society and resulted in repeated and widespread antisemitic riots.

These things die hard. In 1985 President Mitterand commissioned a statue of Dreyfus with the aim of placing it in front of the *École Militaire* where Dreyfus had been expelled from the army in a degrading ritual. The Minister of Defense refused permission to place the statue there.

Mary Pickford was the screen name of Gladys Smith (1892–1979). Known as "America's sweetheart", she was one of the most popular and most highly paid screen stars of the silent era. Like Douglas Fairbanks, she was first brought into the movie industry by D. W. Griffith. She became romantically involved with Fairbanks when the two of them, along with Charlie Chaplin were traveling the country selling war bonds. The two later married. While her screen presence projected innocence and naiveté, she was a formidable business woman in a cutthroat industry.

30 **S'il vous plait . . . Reden Sie? . . . Sprechen Sie? Beloshn ivris? Yesh li . . . proszę panę etc.** Dr Kestleberg speaks French, German, Hebrew, Russian, Polish. It seems the new Messiah would rather speak anything than Yiddish!

Act IV

31 **In unity, there is strenght**: A union slogan. In English, Yiddish and Italian.

32 **Comintern**: The Communist International (1919–1943), an international organisation advocating world communism.

33 **Karl Radek** (1885–1939) Karl Radek would have been well known to the "treyf Bolsheviks" of the Prologue. He was on the famous 1917 sealed train that carried Lenin across Germany in the wake of the February revolution in Russia. He was repeatedly in and out of favour in the Soviet Union. The canonical Karl Radek joke is that three men who share a cell in Soviet Russia are discussing their plights. The first says, "I was imprisoned for attacking Karl Radek." The second says, "But I was imprisoned for defending Karl Radek." The third says, "I am Karl Radek." While in power, he was a leading theoretician, spokesman and propagandist. As a spokesman on foreign affairs he was often quoted abroad. For example, he appears repeatedly in the New York Times during the 1920's and 30's. He was part of the "Left Opposition" during the early 20's when he backed Leon Trotsky. He was expelled from the Communist Party in 1927 when he openly challenged Stalin. He was readmitted after denouncing Trotsky.

At the time of *Messiah in America* in 1933 he was still in power. In 1936 he helped to write the Soviet constitution. Before the end of the year he was convicted of treason and sentenced to ten years hard labour. He was ultimately killed by the NKVD, the predecessor of the KGB.

34 The chicken in question is not simply ignorant of religious doctrine, but is unaware that it's about to be sacrificed.

35 **Koidanov** is small town not far from Minsk in Belarus. It is the historical origin of the Koidanover Hasidim, though no longer its home. In 1932, it was renamed Dzyarzhynsk

in honour of Felix Dzerzhinsky, the founder of the Soviet CHEKA, a forerunner of the KGB.

36 **"What is it"** is a sideshow term of art for such fake creatures as the "Fiji Mermaid" created by stitching an ape's head to the body of a fish.

ACT V

37 The reference is to Chaplin's 1915 film, *The Champion*. It's a striking testimony to the love that audiences felt for The Little Tramp that a 1933 audience would recognize a reference to a 1915 movie.

38 **Tales kotn:** four-cornered fringed garment worn under the shirt by Orthodox Jews.

39 A pun on Rabbi Stephen Wise (sounds like "Weiss", i.e., "white") the leading US reform rabbi of the day and of Temple Emanuel, literally "God with us", whereas "Loy-lonu-el" means "God not with us".

40 **Jess Willard** (1881–1968) won the world heavyweight boxing title from Jack Johnson in 1915 and lost it to Jack Dempsey in 1919. At the time, he was the largest heavyweight champion in boxing history.
   Bob Fitzsimmons (1863–1917) was the lightest world heavyweight champion in boxing history.

41 **Hatikvah:** (lit: "the Hope") Zionist anthem and now the national anthem of the State of Israel. The words were written in 1878 by Naphtali Herz Imber. The tune is based on a sixteenth century Italian song of Giuseppe Cenci. It became the unofficial Israeli anthem in 1948, and was only officially adopted in 2004.

Moyshe Nadir

Born 1885 in Narayiv, Eastern
Galicia (modern day Ukraine)
Moyshe Nadir (Pseudonym
of Yitskhok Rayz / Isaac Reiss) moved to America at the
age of thirteen. Nadir worked
as an insurance agent, window cleaner and sweatshop
worker. From 1902 he began
publishing poetry, satirical
sketches and articles in vari-
ous Yiddish language newspapers and periodicals in New
York.

He wrote and staged vari-
ous plays, translated works
into Yiddish (by writers such as Mark Twain and Eugene
O'Neill) and wrote prolifically for leftist periodicals such as
Morgn Frayhayt, *Hamer* and *Signal*.

His sharply vicious theatre reviews landed Nadir in
trouble with certain theatre agents and so he took to at-
tending performances in disguise.

In 1924 he opened an artists' café, which went out of
business soon afterwards.

Following the Molotov-Ribbentrop Pact in 1939, Nadir
cut off ties with the *Frayhayt* and renounced his pro-Soviet stance.

Moyshe Nadir in English translation

Face to Face, 1920 (Trans. Joseph Kling)
From Man to Man, 2006 (Trans. Harvey Fink)
That Is how it Is, 2008 (Trans. Harvey Fink)

נאַרירם אַ שפּיל מים אַ בלייסצערער

Nadir's self-portrait

Michael Shapiro

Back when hippies roamed the earth, Michael Shapiro moved to the Lower East-Side, down the block from the Peace Eye Bookstore and not far from the old *Frayhayt* building. Then spring came, and he was held up at knife-point and at gunpoint in the course of a single week. He found another place to live. Since then he has followed a veritable dog's breakfast of trades and professions. He has been by turns a street beggar, a household mover, a taxi driver, a piano tuner, a mathematical biologist and a research mathematician. Lately he has been living in a rooming house where the house manager ran off with everybody's cash rent.

His artwork has been collected by the Cambridge (Massachusetts) Public Library's Cambridge Room and Harvard's Woodberry Poetry Room.

His translations have appeared in *Pakn Treger, Jewish Currents* and *In Geveb.*

Self-portrait with tentacles

Farlag Press is an independent publisher run by a collective of translators and literature-lovers. We prioritise translations from stateless and minority languages, as well as the writings of exiles, immigrants and other outsiders.

We are a strictly for-loss company, though we are registered as a non-profit association in France.

www.farlag.com

CPSIA information can be obtained
at www.ICGtesting.com
Printed in the USA
FFHW020631281118
49683954-54059FF